IN THE BEGINNI
THERE WERE

BLOCKHEADS

All of us, at some point in our lives, have laughed at a funny-face toy. We may not remember it, any more than we remember that crazy uncle leaning over our cribs, puffing out his cheeks and bulging his eyes to make us gurgle and flex our fat fingers.

Crazy uncles have always known what toy makers were slower to understand.

Make a funny face at a child, and you win the child's affection.

If you let the child make the funny face ...

Why, then, if you are a toy manufacturer, you not only win the child's affection but goodly profits off the parents, too.

Historically parents have proved eager to keep their children happy. In the later 1800s they shelled out for "Expression Blocks." In the 1920s they shelled out for changeable face blocks. By mid-century they were shelling out for a vegetable "Funny-Face" kit, or a magnetic "Make-A-Face" toy.

The tradition of crazy uncles leaning over the rails of cribs must have had a beginning, now lost in the hazy mists of time. Funny-face toys and make-a-face toys seem to have begun, or at least become commonplace, in the times when toy manufacturing was gaining a firm foothold in America, from the middle to late 19th century.

They came about, in part, because North America had a plentiful supply of wood. Manufacturers of wooden furniture, barrels, and carriages found themselves looking for other, less utilitarian objects to make, and they increasingly turned to producing children's

items. They made doll buggies, child-size wheelbarrows, spinning tops, and, of greatest concern to us here, blocks.

Blocks were traditionally issued in two main categories: building and alphabet. Both were touted as being educational, a matter of concern in 19th-century American house-holds. Building blocks helped children develop coordination and dexterity. Alphabet

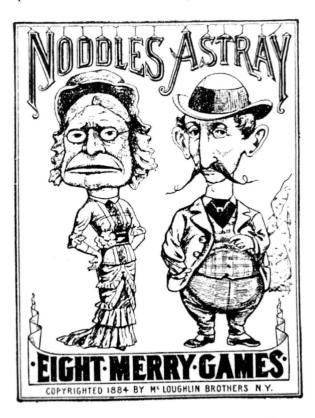

Noddles Astray. McLoughlin Bros. described "Noddles Astray" as a "pack of transformation cards, capable of making over six hundred comical changes." The 52-card set first appeared in 1884. McLoughlin Bros. catalog, 1880s.

Hooray! Hooray! this good team of three
Strain at their bits, and are wild to be free.
With a crack of the whip and lines held tight,
Now we are off like a bird in flight.

Changeable Animals. Game and book publishers offered amusements along the "sliced pictures" line in the later 1800s and early 1900s. Here, a swan and rabbit run along as part of a wagon's harness team ...

Hooray! Hooray! this good team of three
Strain at their bits, and are wild to be free.
With a crack of the whip and lines held tight,
Now we are off like a bird in flight.

... when their heads change to fox and turkey ...

blocks helped teach the foundations of written communication.

Unlike building blocks, which could be made in many shapes and sizes, alphabet blocks tended to be wooden cubes. This meant they had six usable surfaces for displaying letters of the alphabet. Since cubes could be stacked to make stable walls and towers, they could also be used as building blocks. Manufacturers promoted this combined use, as in the "Combination Building and Spelling Blocks," issued by the Brooklyn firm of Westcott in the 1880s and early '90s.

Besides letters of the alphabet, block panels could also show pictures—either small ones entirely contained on one face of a block, or large ones to be assembled by the proper arrangement of several blocks, in puzzle fashion.

These picture faces could be combined with the alphabet blocks, of course, leading to such items as Westcott's "Solid Cube Combination Building, Spelling and Picture Blocks." These cost half a dollar at the time, more than twice as much as the Combination Building and Spelling Blocks."

Picture blocks of a purer sort rivaled building and alphabet blocks in popularity by the late 1800s. In many sets of this sort, all six sides of each block were decorated with parts of pictures. The sets could be assembled into six different complete pictures. In the "Little Folks' Cubes" of the early 1890s, for example, a child could turn the dozen blocks to produce a succession of images: Cinderella, Red Riding Hood, Puss in

■ ■ ■

MANUFACTURERS OF WOODEN FURNITURE, BARRELS, AND CARRIAGES FOUND THEMSELVES LOOKING FOR OTHER, LESS UTILITARIAN OBJECTS TO MAKE, AND THEY INCREASINGLY TURNED TO PRODUCING CHILDREN'S ITEMS.

■ ■ ■

Funny Face!

AN AMUSING HISTORY OF POTATO HEADS, BLOCK HEADS, AND MAGIC WHISKERS

A HISTORY AND VALUE GUIDE
MARK RICH & JEFF POTOCSNAK

Published by

 **krause publications**

700 East State Street • Iola, WI 54990-0001

Please call or write for our free catalog of publications. Our
toll-free number to place an order or obtain a free catalog is
800-258-0929 or please use our regular business telephone
715-445-2214.

Library of Congress Catalog Number: 2001097834
ISBN: 0-87349-418-0

DEDICATION

To the Funny Faces of the World, especially
Elizabeth, Ellen, Sophie, and Stephen

INTRODUCTION

In the Beginning,
There Were Block Heads

CHAPTER 1

Of Magic Whiskers
and Potato Heads

CHAPTER 2

Block Heads

CHAPTER 3

Space Faces and the
Potato-Head Races

CHAPTER 4

Invasion of the
Spud People

Picture Blocks. Early block puzzles took the form of picture blocks.
Each cubical block had a different image on each of its six sides. Each of the six
images was only one part of a larger image, which could be assembled by
properly turning and arranging the whole set of blocks. A set of picture blocks
would feature six different possible images.
These predecessors to changeable blocks still occasionally appear from toy makers,
as did this German set in the 1980s. The uncut pictures to the side show
the scenes to be made. They depict fairy tale scenes, as did many picture
blocks of a century before. Photo by and collection of Mark Rich. 2" by 2½",
Western Germany, 1980s.

Hooray! Hooray! this good team of three
Strain at their bits, and are wild to be free.
With a crack of the whip and lines held tight,
Now we are off like a bird in flight.

... followed by their bodies ...

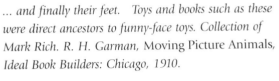

"Will you come and see my home"
Said the Fox one summer day.
"I've a pleasant little dwelling
In the woods not far away."

... and finally their feet. Toys and books such as these were direct ancestors to funny-face toys. Collection of Mark Rich. R. H. Garman, Moving Picture Animals, *Ideal Book Builders: Chicago, 1910.*

Boots, Jack and the Beanstalk, Goody Two Shoes, or the Three Bears.

Picture blocks had European roots. German toy makers were already experts at the production of blocks bearing brightly decorated, color-lithographed sides. While toy makers in America embraced European techniques and approaches, they also began developing their own. Among the leading lights of 19th century toy manufacturing was Pennsylvanian Charles M. Crandall. In the 1870s he was enjoying success with his "Crandall's Building Blocks," which were flat blocks with tongue-and-groove interlocking ends.

At mid-decade he introduced the new "Crandall's Expression Blocks." These alphabet blocks were wooden tiles, not cubes. On one side, the child found a large letter. When the tile was flipped over, part of a wide-eyed face was revealed. It was a "Dissected Picture," or picture puzzle, of that face. Once assembled, the picture must have provoked many smiles, for it showed tiny people crawling over the large face, in *Gulliver's Travels* style.

At the time, Crandall's factories were turning out a steady stream of boxes full of other wooden toys. These also consisted of flat, wooden pieces. Many featured interchangeable parts. With the "Acrobats," children could assemble acrobats with the arms, heads, and legs in their proper places—or not, according to their whim. With the "Menagerie," children could put animals together the expected way, or create unusual combinations instead.

Blocks depicting an unusual human face ...

And put-together toys with interchangeable parts ...

Neither kind of toy was quite a funny-face or make-a-face toy.

Yet the stage was set.

Within fifty years, "Ole' Million Face Changeable Blocks" would appear. Not only a changeable-face toy, it would prove to be a changeable-name toy, becoming "Changeable Charlie" twenty-three years farther down the road, soon after the end of World War II.

Four years after that, a funny-face toy involving potatoes arrived on the scene, and met with almost overnight success.

Three years after that, to the delight of young shavers everywhere, magic whiskers arrived.

A Funny Face Toy. The "Mr. Potato Head" kits of 1952 proved a success, much more so than Hassenfeld Bros., the pencil-making parent company, anticipated. This rare, original store display fell out of a stack of old Life magazines. Collection of Jeff Potocsnak. Hassenfeld Bros. store display, 1952.

CHAPTER 1

REMEMBER THE PROMISE? "THE BEST FRIEND A BOY OR GIRL COULD EVER HAVE."

*Best friend or not, boys and girls grabbed these toys from store shelves—
or had parents doing the grabbing for them—by the millions.
Part of the joy came in packages of little plastic eyes, noses, ears,
and mouths. The rest of it came from the root cellar, the vegetable bin
of the refrigerator, or right out of the garden:
They could be carrots, apples, onions, beets, or cucumbers.
Best of all, they could be potatoes.*

Funny-face toys gradually became more common as the toy industry thrived and expanded in the 1920s, and again in the 1930s in the aftermath of the Great Depression. Some were made of wood, while others appeared in paper and cardboard. American Toy Works, a firm that started in New York City in the 1920s, was issuing "cut-out funny faces sets" by the late 1930s. The sets included one called "A Million Funny Faces." Many sets came in the form of "Santa Claus surprise packages."

Such inexpensive toys could still be produced during the mid-1940s, for the pleasure of wartime children.

While rubber and various metals were being rationed, and their use in toys restricted, the traditional materials of wood, paper, and cardboard saw continued and even expanded use by toy manufacturers. In the years following the war, restrictions only gradually eased and the supply of materials slowly returned to normal. It was only fitting that the first postwar funny-face toy to make waves, "Changeable Charlie," should be a

Infinite Possibilities. While Mr. Potato Head would eventually be diminished into a toy with one particular look, the toy that became a household name had incredible flexibility. Faces depicted any and every possible human expression and facial type. Here a potato has a vaguely bandito appearance. Photo by Mark Rich.

Mr. Cyclops Head. Photo by Mark Rich.

Mr. Gourd Head. Photo by Mark Rich.

Mr. Smart Guy. Photo by Mark Rich.

12

wood-and-paper toy, and in fact a block toy.

Plastic first appeared as a toy-making material in the later 1930s. Not being restricted during World War II, it gradually saw increasing use through the 1940s. By the time the first Baby Boom children were playing with their first toys, the idea of giving a child a plaything of colorful, hygienic plastic was no longer surprising or unusual.

Manufacturers soon realized the new material was perfect for premiums. Premiums were among the cheapest of all toys—so cheap, in fact, they were given away free as promotional incentives. The Cracker Jack Company, which had used celluloid in some prewar prize items, began using modern plastics for its "prize" toys in 1946, immediately after World War II. Children, previously used to pulling die-cast, tin-litho, or paper toys out of their confection packages, began finding colored plastic animals, tractors, and racing cars.

A designer of toys and premiums, George Lerner of Brooklyn, New York, came up with a toy set he called the "Identikit." It consisted of an envelope of plastic pieces. Each piece was the shape of a facial feature or accessory, such as an eye, nose, hat, or mouth. From the back of these pieces, plastic spikes protruded, so the pieces could be stuck into a vegetable or fruit of the child's choice. Lerner sold the idea to a cereal company, which used it in a routine promotion. The firm probably thought in terms of fruit: the eyes and noses would look friendly and funny sticking out of an apple, orange, or banana at the breakfast table.

Yet George Lerner thought this toy set would be entertaining if used in any fruit or vegetable. He believed it had more potential. He visited different toy companies with his idea, trying to extend the toy's life.

The big manufacturers, all of them having offices in New York City, must have turned him down in 1951. Lerner's plastic and flannel pieces, in the shape of eyes, hats, noses, eyebrows, mustaches, mouths, pipes, hair, and eyeglasses, would make their reappearance. Yet, when they did so the next year, in charming, yellow boxes, they were issued by one of the newest and smallest players in the industry.

If twenty observers had been asked which toy companies would have big hits that season, they could have rattled off a hundred or more top companies without ever thinking of Hassenfeld Brothers. Even the Hassenfelds might not have named Hassenfeld Brothers. While they obviously saw something the rest of the toy industry did not, they reacted cautiously to Lerner's idea. They felt insecure enough about the proposition to offer the toy inventor only a five hundred dollar advance against royalties.

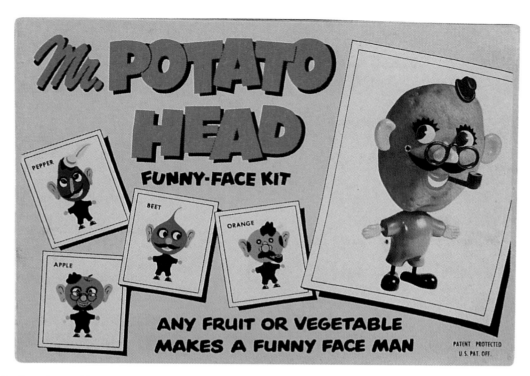

Any Fruit or Vegetable. The original yellow box emphasized the toy's potato incarnation, but also featured other fruits and vegetables: orange, apple, onion, and green pepper. The kit boxes measured 10½" by 7". Collection of Jeff Potocsnak. "Mr. Potato Head Funny-Face Kit," Hassenfeld Bros., 1952.

THE YEAR 1952

In some ways, Hassenfeld Brothers' "Mr. Potato Head Funny Face Kit" made its debut on a ready-made stage.

Since the war, the population of children in the country had jumped with each passing year. The time from 1946 to 1947 alone saw an increase of over a million in the number of children under five years of age. Another half-million increase followed the next year, followed by another three-quarters of a million by 1949. A second three-quarters of a million leap followed by 1950. The babies kept arriving, so that in the years 1951 and 1952, the number of children under age five stood at just over seventeen million, a figure three-quarters higher than it had been before the war.

The Hassenfelds were looking for ideas for their toy line for good reason. The country had more children in more play rooms and more kindergartens than ever before. Many of those 1.2 million kids born from 1946 to 1947, the first Baby Boom kids, stood on the verge of first-grade.

Meanwhile, alongside the birthrate, the country's wealth had also been steadily rising. While census estimates put the amount of net disposable personal income across the country at just over ninety-two billion dollars immediately before the war, the figure had risen to over two hundred and twenty-five billion by 1952. Not only did the country have children arriving by the basket load, it had parents practically standing in line to spend hard-earned money on playthings, whether toys for the kids or recreational equipment for themselves. Manufacturers could expect a sizeable portion of that nearly quarter-trillion dollars of disposable income. United States families would spend almost a billion and a half, just so they and their kids could have fun.

Toy manufacturers were doing their best to supply the country with interesting playthings. The scene in 1951 bustled with activity as hundreds of manufacturers, new and old, jostled to gain prominence and establish their goods as exemplary and desirable. Yet so large was the postwar crop of children that if a company could introduce a new toy essentially sound in concept and execution, that company could expect at least a modicum of success.

14

Dump Truck. *Structo Mfg. Co.,* Billy and Ruth *1952 catalog.*

"Bobo." Doughboy Industries, Toy Fair *for 1951 catalog.*

■ ■ ■

The stage on which
Mr. Potato Head made his
debut was far from an empty
one. Hundreds of companies
were issuing high-profile toys
in the early 1950s, in every
conceivable category.

■ ■ ■

"Electric Football Game." Tudor Metal Products Corp., Billy and Ruth *1952 catalog.*

Road Grader. *Charles William Doepke Manufacturing Company,* Toy Fair *for 1951 catalog.*

BEFORE THE CURTAIN RAISED

Hassenfield Brothers' "Mr. Potato Head" appeared on the scene when the toy-manufacturing world was entering its most competitive stage. Dozens, if not hundreds, of manufacturer names and brand names were already familiar to five-and-dime and department store retailers and customers. Dozens, if not hundreds, more entered the fray in the 1951 to 1952 season, as new companies jostled for position in the market.

Even among industry leaders, the list of well-known toys that season was a long one. American Metal Specialties Corp. was enjoying success with its "Doll-E-Bath" and other doll accessories and furniture; Argo Industries, with its "Action Car" sets; Banner Plastics Corp., with its "Metaltone" plastic flatware, kiddie jewelry, and small plastic toy vehicles; Banthrico Industries, with 1:25 die-cast scale models of contemporary cars, with spring motors; and Milton Bradley with "Hopalong Cassidy" and "Uncle Wiggly" games.

Several firms, including T. Cohn, De Luxe Game Corporation, Kiddie Joy Playthings Company, Louis Marx & Company, and Ranger Steel Products Corporation, issued popular play sets involving colorful tin buildings and plastic play pieces.

Coleman & Morris, Emenee Industries, Magnus Harmonic Corporation, Mattel, and Pressman Toy Corporation made their names with musical toys of all kinds. Courtland Manufacturing Company, Louis Marx & Company, and Structo Manufacturing Company enjoyed success with pressed steel and tin toy trucks; the Charles William Doepke Manufacturing Company and Ny-Lint Tool & Manufacturing Company, with heavy-duty toy construction equipment; Doughboy Industries, with its famous fifty-inch "Bobo Punching Clown"; and Electric Game Company, with such flashing-light attractions as "Electric Bunny Run," "Electric Fire Fighters," and "Electric Football."

Empire Plastic Corporation was busily issuing its sets of miniature plastic cars, trucks, and airplanes; Esquire Novelty Company, its Western outfits; Gaston Manufacturing Company, its changeable block toys; and Goldberger Doll Corporation, Ideal Toy Corporation, and Midwestern Manufacturing Company, their popular-priced dolls. Gotham Pressed Steel and Burrowes Corporations competed at producing children's pool tables.

Halsam Products Company had success with wooden "American Logs" and "American Bricks" sets, and diverse block sets; Hewell Manufacturing Company, with its ping-pong-ball-shooting air guns; Ideal Toy Corp, with plastic pantry sets, "Twisty Bear" flexible plush bears, plastic vehicle toys, and plastic soldiers; James Industries, with "Slinky," Little Tot Toy Company, with vinyl stuffed animals and washable clown dolls; Model Craft, with "Alice in Wonderland" and other activity kits; and Nosco Plastics, with plastic hot rods whose transparent engine cowls revealed "working" pistons.

Parker Brothers enjoyed continuing prosperity with "Monopoly"; Pressman Toy Corporation, with peg and slate kits, doctor and nurse bags, magnetic dart games, and blackboards; Rich Industries, with wooden rocking horses and shooflys; Saalfield Publishing and Stencil Art Publishing Companies, with activity and stencil books; and O. Schoenhut with children's grand pianos.

Selco Novelty Products Co. flourished with its "Marksman" dart pistols; Toy Tinkers, with "Wonder Tinkertoys"; Unique Art and Louis Marx & Company, with mechanical tin toys; and Wolverine Supply & Manufacturing Company, with toy ironing boards and kitchen appliances, the plastic "Sulky Racer," and tin pull-trains.

Hassenfeld Brothers itself had won significant stature in the crowded toy-manufacturing field with its doctor and nurse kits, "Beaux Arts" paint sets, blackboard and pencil sets, "Junior Miss" sewing kits, and the "Alice in Wonderland" make-up kit.

As diverse and numerous as the above toys and companies might seem, they made up only a fraction of the total. An observer might have thought no room remained for new toys, or new companies. Yet more of both would arrive through the Baby Boom years, as would new babies, day after day, month after month, and year after year.

Mr. Melon Head. Photo by Mark Rich.

Apple Man. Photo by Mark Rich.

Thoughtful Mug. Photo by Mark Rich.

If the idea was exciting and new, the company could hope for more. When the Hassenfelds saw the "Identikit," they had enough familiarity with the manufacturing scene to know Lerner had come up with something markedly different from anything yet available.

On the one hand, they could have just copied the idea. They operated within a milieu in which nothing could be more normal than simply to steal a good idea. If one company had success with pegboards or blackboards, others followed suit. If one season saw sales soar for new vinyl-faced dolls, other doll makers lost no time. Certain concepts could not be patented, or at least patented with any hope of locking out the competition.

Other toy companies might easily have taken the stance that once someone started manufacturing the "Identikit," the idea was out of the closet, and now ripe for harvest and for capitalizing upon with look-alike products. Yet the Hassenfelds had enough insight to see longer-term possibilities for this "Identikit." While they might not have seen the kit turning into a property that would help sustain a major corporation for fifty years and more, they clearly did see it as one of potentially significant value, and as one worth acquiring by legal, above-the-table transactions. Only that way, after all, would they be able to defend the idea from other copycats.

They also saw it as an item worthy of doing some experimenting with, in terms of advertising. The company assembled some print ads, and they put together some film ads through a few local stations, for airing on the new medium of television. By 1953, these ads, especially the commercials on the popular *The Jackie Gleason Show*, made Mr. Potato Head almost a household name.

OF PENCIL BOXES AND DOCTOR KITS

Ironically, Hassenfeld Brothers itself joined the field of toy manufacturers through copy-cat methods. Hillel and Henry Hassenfeld, who formed a scrap textile company in the 1910s in Providence, Rhode Island, began manufacturing pencil boxes in the 1920s. To help sales, the company began filling its "Gilt Edge" boxes with rulers, pencils, and other school supplies. It bought filler from other manufacturers at first, and then moved into pencil making. While not yet among the leading producers of such "school companions"—those firms were American Manufacturing Concern of Falconer, New York, and Eagle Pencil and Goody Manufacturing Companies of New York City—Hassenfeld Brothers enjoyed success, and continued moving into new areas. It required little imagination to move from school-companion filler to art-set filler: paints, modeling clay, and

Mr. Cardboard Head. During the first few months of the toy's release, a child opening a "Mr. Potato Head" kit would discover a figure with a cardboard potato for a head. The cardboard head held an assortment of face pieces in place. Collection of Jeff Potocsnak. "Mr. Potato Head Funny-Face Kit," Hassenfeld Bros., 1952.

crayons. The firm also promoted the new art sets, which appeared by the late 1930s, under the "Gilt Edge" name.

Henry's son Merrill, who joined the firm as a salesman shortly before World War II, saw what other companies had hit upon as a winning idea—toy doctor and nurse kits. Instead of pencils or craft supplies, these sets contained toy stethoscopes, medicine bottles, thermometers, and syringes.

In the post Great Depression years, companies including Fleischaker & Baum and Hale-Nass Corporation, both of New York City, and Jackson-Guldan Violin Company and Wicker Toy Manufacturing Company, both of Columbus, Ohio, were making toy medical sets and doctor's bags. The popular items sold through dime stores, department stores, and catalog outfits. By the late 1930s, New York City's Transogram Company, which had already been making toy suitcases and various boxed toy sets, joined them and issued "Little Country" doctor kits. Brinkman Engineering Company of Dayton, Ohio, and James McGowan Associates of New York City likewise began supplying would-be doctors and nurses with appropriate equipment.

While Hassenfeld Brothers was late in jumping on the bandwagon, the firm already had its foot in the toy-manufacturing door thanks to its art sets. It had already made the connections and established the distribution channels that would help it re-position itself as a maker of toys. The

■■■

"EVERY IRISHMAN, THE SAYING GOES, HAS A POTATO IN HIS HEAD."

JULIUS CHARLES HARE (1795-1854) AND AUGUST WILLIAM HARE (1792-1834), GUESS AT TRUTH, 1827.

■■■

Mr. Foam Head. Switching from a cardboard to foam head probably helped speed up packaging, as demand for the kits increased. The change took place within months of the toy's debut. Otherwise the kits remained the same. Collection of Jeff Potocsnak. "Mr. Potato Head Funny-Face Kit," Hassenfeld Bros., 1952.

18

Mr. Surrealist Head. *Much as the Surrealist game "Exquisite Corpse" was kin to such commercial products as "'Ole' Million Faces," Surrealist painting and sculpture were near kin to "Mr. Potato Head" kits. Since the kits were marketed, in part, as a way of making clever party centerpieces, they often fell subject to adult play. Children were equally capable of improvising Surrealist images, however, since images of European paintings often appeared in the popular press. Photo by Mark Rich.*

UNCLE SAM FIGHTERSET
★ ★ ★

"Uncle Sam Fighterset." Hassenfeld Bros. advertisement, Toys and Novelties, *March 1943.*

company maintained display rooms through wartime in New York City's Fifth Avenue "Toy Building," along with a couple hundred other toy manufacturers. It promoted its entire line of pencils, pencil boxes, school bags, scrapbooks, photo albums, paint and crayon sets, and now the doctor and nurse kits. As before, the new toys were issued as "Gilt Edge Play Sets."

The young Merrill Hassenfeld, moreover, showed good marketing sense. Much as other companies were adapting their toy lines to wartime conditions, he helped develop a line suited not only to Hassenfeld Brothers' production capabilities, but also to the new needs of the country's playrooms. "Wartime Is Still Playtime for America's Children," announced one of Hassenfeld's advertisements for 1943. The company successfully introduced not only its "De Luxe Junior Doctor Kit" and "De Luxe Nurse's Kit," but also two kits uniquely suited to the times: the "Junior Air Raid Warden Set" and "Junior WAAC Set."

Merrill Hassenfeld also assisted in two other moves designed to take the company deeper into toyland.

In years to come, an important part of the Hassenfeld Brothers toy line, to be dubbed "Hasbro" toys by the early 1950s, would be kits for girls wanting to play house in the most adult way possible. Most notable among these would be the cosmetic, sewing, and embroidery kits, which would be issued by the 1950s in the "Junior Miss" line. In 1943, this segment of Hassenfeld Brothers' toy-manufacturing activity was inaugurated with the release of the first "Dolly's Homemaker" sets for young girls.

The company also released the "Uncle Sam Fighterset," a paper toy featuring "three-dimensional units of Army, Navy, and Air Corps." While such play sets would have a relatively small role in the future Hasbro toy line, the company would soon be issuing a number of make-believe toy sets, which would include small, figural elements, in the "Let's Play" series. Some of the plastic play pieces developed by the mid-1950s, including small plastic toy ambulances, dairy trucks, and fire engines, would see use in both games and play sets.

A similar effort to tie into children's interest in the war resulted in an item billed energetically as "Not a toy! Not a game!" The "Service Writing Portfolio Kits" arose as direct outgrowths of Hassenfeld Brothers' experience in school-companion production, adapted to wartime.

Merrill Hassenfeld was made president of Hassenfeld Brothers for his work in successfully guiding the company into the realm of toy manufacturing. Yet nothing he developed ventured far from the company's origins in pencil-box making.

It took someone from outside the pencil-box field to see outside the box.

FUNNY FACE MAN

For all its originality, one common thread did tie Hassenfeld Brothers' new "Mr. Potato Head" kit to its prior kits.

All the company's products, from the 1920s through the 1940s, were accessories. The pencil boxes were literally called "school companions" by the trade. They were accessories for learning. The crayon and paint sets were another kind of school companion, and were also meaningless without paper or boards, which the company only began providing in the 1950s when the paint-by-number and color-by-number fads were getting underway. The doctor and nurse kits at root were accessories for dolls, as doll maker Fleischaker & Baum realized in making its toy medical sets. So were the sewing sets, as was made especially clear in the 1950s Hasbro sets that included one or more small plastic dolls in need of clothing.

As with those, so with the "Mr. Potato Head Funny Face Kit."

Lerner saw clearly, for the first time, that a plaything existed in every household refrigerator, and even on every dinner table.

Everyone played with food, at some point in their lives.

The universality of the injunction spoken in every American household to each child, at least once, proved as much: "Don't play with your food!"

No toy companies had capitalized on this fact, and for good reason. America in the 1930s was emerging from the devastating Great Depression.

Food manufacturers could encourage people to use their products through promotions and give-aways, and could issue such toy-like items as "Skippy" cereal bowls and "Radio Orphan Annie Shake-Ups" for mixing Ovaltine. Yet they could not be so audacious as to suggest that kids play with their food.

Companies could tell parents to drink Arbuckle Brothers coffee so their children could have Jack and Jill rag dolls. They could encourage kids to beg for Merita Bread and Wheaties, so they could be first on their block with Lone Ranger and Tonto posters and premiums. Yet they could never say, "Kids, play

MORE AND MORE PEOPLE ACROSS THE NATION ARE ACCEPTING THE CORDIAL INVITATION TO

Meet Mr. Spudnut

COAST TO COAST . . ALASKA TO MEXICO

SPUDNUTS*

Meet Mr. Spudnut. *George Lerner's idea was not entirely new in the industry. The idea of personifying a food product had happened before, in the advertising industry. Particularly evocative of the later Mr. Potato Head was Mr. Spudnut, a doughnut-man with cheerful face, top hat, bow tie, and cane. Made by Pelton's Spudnuts in the 1940s, the doughnuts were sold only in "the Genuine Mr. Spudnut Bag." Far from being a limited-exposure campaign, Spudnuts were distributed nationally, and were being advertised in* Life *several years before Mr. Potato Head made his debut. The confection also had a tellingly similar name. Pelton's Spudnuts ad,* Life, *1949.*

Potato Head Blues. *Jazz great Louis Armstrong recorded his jaunty and upbeat composition "Potato Head Blues" in Chicago in 1927 with the Hot Seven, one of the most important and influential bands of the time. The 3-minute, 55-second recording featured solos by Armstrong and Johnny Dodds on clarinet, over the characteristic straight-chopping rhythm section led by Lil Armstrong on piano. Collection of Jeff Potocsnak. 78 record label, R2185 Parlophone, England.*

20

with your food."

Wartime shortages and rationing only made the situation worse. Yet, in its way, that worsening may have worked in Lerner's and the Hassenfelds' favor. Children always like to play with whatever is on hand. Barring something from play gives it the unbearable attraction of the forbidden. As a consequence, every child's natural but rebellious urge to play with food had been bottled year after year.

By the early 1950s, despite worries about the Bomb and the Russians, Americans were relaxing and enjoying themselves. They were buying fancy new cars, flocking to drive-ins, and cooking hamburgers on their backyard grills without saving the grease for explosives.

Were they relaxing so far as to play with their food? No. Kids were still being told not to.

Then, for their birthdays and parties and Christmases, they were being given kits designed to enable them to do just that. Lerner, in realizing that a toy existed in every vegetable bin, realized that kids only needed the merest encouragement, in the form of accessories for those vegetables.

Is it any wonder the toy was an immediate success?

MAGIC WHISKERS

It may be in the nature of funny-face toys to come out of the blue and enjoy unexpected success.

Three years after the debut of the "Mr. Potato Head Funny-Face Kit," Smethport Specialty Company of Smethport, Pennsylvania, took examples of its own new funny-face toy to Woolworth's, pioneer of five-and-dime mass-selling of low-priced goods.

Smethport had a strong working relationship with Woolworth's, one that extended over thirty years. In fact, the firm owed its initial success in the 1920s to F. W. Woolworth's support. This fact alone might have suggested to the chain, had it given the matter a second's thought, that the name of the new toy, "Wooly Willy," could have been chosen as a tribute, at least in part.

Yet Woolworth's, whether flattered or not, turned down the toy as unlikely to interest anyone.

After some effort, Smethport Specialty talked a reluctant buyer for the G. C. Murphy five-and-dime chain into trying six dozen, which then went up for sale in Indianapolis.

It was apparently a whim on the buyer's part. He believed the things, true to their name, would gather wool.

Yet the six dozen sold out in days.

A subsequent order of 12,000 sets sold out in weeks.

Woolworth's and other five-and-dimes readily admitted their mistakes, and helped launch "Wooly Willy, the Magnetic

Pure Attractiveness. Marvel and Smethport Specialty used these lithographed metal toys in "Electric Acrobats" and other toy sets, together with a small horseshoe magnet, which would "animate" the clowns and horseback riders. Today "Cracker Jack" collectors seek these colorful items, since they were also used as prizes in that popular confection and possibly in "Checkers," the rival confection. Not issued by Marvel or Smethport, they may have been made by Dowst Mfg. Co. or another 1920s-1940s toy manufacturer with tinplate capacity. Photo by and collection of Mark Rich.

Personality—Change His Character with the Wand" toward widespread success. It would become one of the best-selling toys of the Baby Boom years.

The toy's roots went back to 1923, when Ralph Herzog and William Kerr founded Marvel Specialty Company. The enterprising pair manufactured magnets from high-carbon steel, and packaged them with attractively lithographed sheet-metal clowns and horseback riders.

The idea behind the fledgling company's first and second toys, "Electric Acrobats" and "Electric Toy Set," was simple. A child could use the horseshoe magnet to lift the tin-plate clown off the table, without touching magnet to clown, and then make the colorful clown spin circles by a few manipulations of the magnet. In the case of the horse and rider, the child could make the horse rear on its hind legs. The sets of toys, stitched onto display cards, were also released as the "American Magnet Electric Acrobat Toy Set."

The company moved out of its barn fairly quickly, thanks to the F. W. Woolworth Company buying much of its output. Marvel Specialty expanded its range to include spinning toys, notably the "Twin Racing Tops," the "Flicker Top," and celluloid pinwheels. Sales remained strong enough to keep the company in business through the Great Depression. The firm moved to a new location in the early 1930s, changing its name to Smethport Specialty Company at the departure of original partner William Kerr.

Toy production ceased entirely during World War II and the years immediately afterward, when the supply of materials was slow to return to normal. Smethport Specialty did begin re-emphasizing toys in the early 1950s, thanks in part to the two younger Herzogs, Donald and James, who joined the company.

Naturally enough, the basic notion behind "Wooly Willy" had been kicking around the Smethport factory for some time. After all, the company had plenty of magnetic dust around, leftovers from the constant manufacture of magnets for magnetic toys. It also, of course, had magnets.

The missing element was an airtight container that would hold the filings in place and

21

The Magnetic Man. A significantly larger magic-whiskers toy made by Smethport went by the name "Dapper Dan, the Magnetic Man." Instead of a Magic Wand, these sets came with a "powerful magnetic pencil," which was a three-inch wooden rod with a heavy magnet fixed to one end. Unlike Wooly Willy, Dapper Dan's face came without eyebrows. The bigger size made this a slightly easier toy to master. Another large magnetic drawing toy by the same company was "Doodle Balls," which employed ball bearings instead of magnetic filings. Photo by and collection of Mark Rich. 14" by 10½", Smethport Specialty Co., 1950s.

Dime Store Cowboy. The manufacturing techniques that made cheap plastic cowboy figures possible also made "Mr. Potato Head" kits possible. Plastic-injection molding gave rise to countless dime store toys in the 1950s, especially Western figures of cowboys and Indians. This large cowboy, 6½" tall when atop his horse and 6½" from nose to tip of tail, was made by Payton Products. The New York firm made similar Indian, 7th Cavalry, Robin Hood, Arab, and Foreign Legion figures. Photo by and collection of Mark Rich.

Magnetic Personality. The second funny-face toy sensation of the 1950s would become almost as well known among the generation raised on dime-store toy fare as "Mr. Potato Head." "Wooly Willy" appeared on store shelves in 1955, after a gestation period that may have gone back twenty years.

The original 29-cent price appears stamped to the left of Willy's face. Artist Leonard Mackowski's signature appears on the back of the card, next to the drawing of a mushroom. Collection of Jeff Potocsnak; photo by Mark Rich. 7" by 9", Smethport Specialty Co., 1955.

still allow them to be seen. The plastic-molding techniques and materials of the 1930s had been inadequate to the task. The U.S. Army, however, developed a means of vacuum-forming plastic sheets by the early 1950s. The process turned out to be perfect for making air-tight and low-static containers of clear plastic.

Artist Leonard Mackowski of Bradford, Pennyslvania, drew the now-familiar wool-less Willy face on the playing board. In its original form, it was tinted orange over a yellow background. He also drew the elves and children around the edges and added attractive sketches on the back of the card, depicting some of Willy's transformations with fanciful names: Harry the Hermit, Dick the Dude, Pete the Pirate, and Charlie the Clown.

"Wooly Willy is a shifty character," said the blurbs on the back of the cards, which remained largely unchanged from their introduction through the end of the Baby Boom years. "His many disguises completely change his appearance."

"Wooly Willy" occupied the bargain-toy slot at twenty-nine cents. The larger "Dapper Dan," for children who needed a bigger canvas for their magnetic-hair brushes, cost all of a dollar.

While the toy ended up serving a multitude of roles during its heyday, such as light-hearted promotional items during the campaigns of bald candidates for office, "Wooly Willy" will be best remembered as an absorbing toy for many a sleepy afternoon.

IT LOOKED SO EASY

Y ou tended to say the same thing after a few minutes with Smethport Specialty's "Wooly Willy" as you did after picking up Ohio Art's 1960s hit, "Etch A Sketch":

"But it looked so easy!"

When you picked up the Magic Wand, you managed to get the first bit of eyebrow where you wanted. Then you worked on the second eyebrow, only to find the first eyebrow was now moving closer to the second.

So you learned to hold the Magic Wand a little away from the plastic, for a little finer control. The magnetic filings, however, tended to resist your control, when they were sitting in big masses. Eventually, though, you learned to break it up into more manageable masses. You also figured out to fine-tune things by using the Magic Wand under the board.

Then you had a beautiful portrait of an acceptably hairy guy—except for those stray metal filings here and there, looking like stubble.

So you picked up the "Wooly Willy" to shake those stray filings down to the bottom, to clean things up and tidy the image—only to have all the filings slip away from Willy's face. It was almost impossible to remember that nothing held those eyebrows and whiskers in place, once situated by the Magic Wand.

So then you had to start all over again.

Wooly Willy as Davy Crockett. *Photo by Mark Rich.*

Mean-Looking but Smiling. *Photo by Mark Rich.*

24

"'Ole' Million Face." One of the greatest of funny-face toys appeared in the 1920s. Here,
its pieces lay scattered, showing both tops and front sides of the blocks. Children could play
with the pieces as they sat within the box, keeping the image arranged neatly. They could
also play with them outside the box, stacking or otherwise arranging them, and devising
even odder faces. One of the most striking face images in American toy history, *"'Ole'
Million Face"* was drawn by illustrator and Pulitzer Prize-winner Carey Orr
(1890–1967). Photo by and collection of Mark Rich. A. Schoenhut Company, 1925.

CHAPTER 2

TURN A BLOCK: SMILE!
TURN ANOTHER: BLACK EYE!
TURN YET ANOTHER: LUMP ON THE HEAD!

Was a playroom of the '50s, '60s, or '70s
complete without a set of "Changeable" blocks?
Millions of Baby Boom kids grew up playing with these toys.
And children of the Great Depression years
played with an almost identical toy.

The idea for interchangeable picture blocks with funny human faces could have come from any one of the dozens of block and toy companies operating in the later 1800s and earlier 1900s.

Did Charles M. Crandall first make the innovation? Was it one of the other toy inventors in the extended Crandall families of the 1800s?

Or did the idea come from McLoughlin Brothers of New York, which was responsible for the "Aunt Louisa Cube Puzzles," picture puzzles made of thirty cubes each, and also for "Noddles Astray," which featured faces and bodies on cards "capable of making over six hundred comical changes"? McLoughlin also was issuing figural block toys by the 1880s. By stacking three "Comic Cubes" blocks, one showing a head, the next a torso, and last the legs, a child could assemble a quick succession of "perfect figures." The set contained six cubes, leading to "several hundred changes," the manufacturer promised.

Or did the idea arise at one of the dozens of smaller American manufacturers who issued toy books, toy blocks, block figures, and "dissected pictures" in the 1870s, 1880s, and 1890s?

Certainly, too, European toy makers cannot be dismissed. By the mid-1800s, English children could play with card sets

of "Changeable Gentleman," in which different profiles were sliced in three interchangeable parts. Undoubtedly, children across the continent played with similar paper toys.

Another distinct American possibility, however, is that early giant of the toy manufacturing world, Albert Schoenhut. An industrious German immigrant, he established the A. Schoenhut Company in Philadelphia in 1872, five years after Crandall established himself in Covington, Pennsylvania. The firm appears to have been under the reins of William G. Schoenhut by the 1920s, when the company released what seems to have been the first changeable-block funny-face toy to acquire significant national fame.

While the Schoenhut company was entering its last decade when it released the toy, it was by no means fading into quiet senescence. It continued to release new toys through the end of the 1920s. Yet, when it manufactured its changeable-block, funny-face toy, the blocks bore the name of someone who was clearly not an employee of the company. He was also not someone normally thought of as a toy designer.

The toy itself was "'Ole' Million Face Changeable Blocks." The Face Corporation, another Philadelphia company that was the toy's licensee and distributor, apparently had an

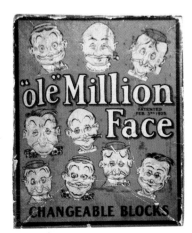

arrangement with Schoenhut, enabling it to market and sell the item.

The copyright was held by Carey Orr.

Historians of the political cartoon know the name well. As an illustrator, the Tennessee-born Orr made his name with political cartoons for the *Chicago Tribune* in the years before World War II. He continued with the newspaper well afterwards, earning a Pulitzer in 1961 for his distinguished career. In his earlier years, he apparently did work outside the sphere of political cartooning and may have been among Walt Disney's instructors at the Academy of Fine Arts in Chicago.

He also plainly dabbled in the design of playthings.

A complex toy, his "'Ole' Million Face Changeable Blocks" set consisted of eleven blocks in four different sizes. To make a picture eight inches tall by six inches across, Orr arranged the blocks in five rows. The bottom and top blocks extended the full length across. The second-to-bottom blocks were cut in thirds; the middle-row blocks, in quarters; and the next-to-top blocks, in halves.

The arrangement suited the subject well.

One of a Million. *A person could steadily keep changing "'Ole' Million Face" and never see exactly the same face twice. Changing one block per second, twenty four hours per day, would mean working through the permutations of the toy in about a month and a half. Photo by and collection of Mark Rich. 6" by 8", "'Ole' Million Face," A. Schoenhut Company, 1925.*

Changeable Animals. *"One Thousand Jolly Cats and Dogs" featured nine wooden cubes, two and a half inches square. "They have heads, bodies, and feet of cats in grotesque attire and positions on the different blocks," said a Marshall Field & Co. catalog advertisement in 1892. "These fit together and make innumerable comical combinations." Game possibly by McLoughlin Bros., New York.*

Orr used the top block to show the top of the head. It could be bald or not. It could wear a bowler or straw hat. The next two blocks down featured the pair of eyebrows, arched in various degrees of pleasure, anger, or dismay. The middle blocks fell in a natural order, from left to right: left ear, then left eye, then right eye, and finally right ear. Orr drew the ears of several kinds, and added criss-crossing cheekbone bandages or anxious sweat-drops in a few images. He drew various eyes, including wide-open surprised, crossed, and bruised-shut from a punch.

Like many comic-face toys, the nose provided a fine point of focus. Occupying the middle block of that second-to-bottom row, it ranged from real honker with off-center wart, to modestly mustachioed beak. Orr drew the cheek blocks to each side to include the curved ends of the wide mouth, in various exaggerated grins and frowns. To the cheek on the right-hand block, he added two then-obligatory options: a cigar, with its label turned up, and a corncob pipe.

The bottom block most conveyed the gentleman's style. "Ole" Million Face could wear a conservative suit with be-flowered lapel, a wilder outfit with spotted tie and diamond stud underneath, or a shirt with stiffly upright collar. The fourth option showed no neck or shoulders, but only a bare chin with a white beard growing under the edge, in Old World style. These varied chins conveyed almost as much character as did the noses.

A funny-face toy, and definitely a simply funny toy, "'Ole' Million Face" had the wiry, highly exaggerated features to be found in earlier 20th century cartooning. All the bemused children lucky enough to have one must have spent hours with it, and must have worked out, between them, all 4,194,304 permutations.

The A. Schoenhut Company did appear a healthy company in the 1920s. Its predominantly wooden toys consisted of musical toys, especially pianos and metallophones, "Humpty-Dumpty" circus toys, dollhouses, exercisers, toy sailboats, and doll furniture. It also made nested blocks, "colored wagon blocks," and the "Little Tots" building blocks.

The firm managed to survive the onset of the Great Depression and early years of recovery, only to close its doors in 1935. If it had not already folded, the Face Corporation likely shared the larger firm's fate.

In any case, "'Ole' Million Face" appears to have vanished from the toy manufacturing map until after World War II had come and gone. Carey Orr's funny-face toy would then reappear. It would appear slightly freshened up, and would bear a new name.

The new version would become even more famous than the old.

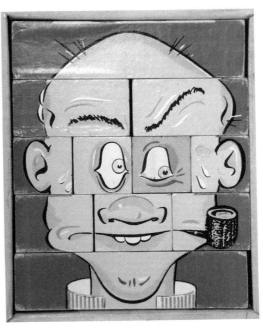

CHANGEABLE CHARLIE

For children of the postwar years, no block toys are as beloved as "Changeable Charlie," a block set issued by a succession of companies through the Baby Boom years.

From 1948 through much of the 1950s, Gaston Manufacturing Company of Cincinnati, Ohio, featured "Changeable Charlie Changeable Blocks" as the headliner of its "Changeable Blocks" line. Gaston then expanded the range of make-a-face block toys, bringing in some of the most famous

Ole' 4,194,304 Faces. While he appeared under other names, the "Changeable Charlie" name bestowed on this 11-block set by Gaston Manufacturing Co. became the one everyone knew. The blocks shown here were issued by Halsam, the third successive company to use the "Changeable Charlie" name on the toy. Halsam dropped the "Changeable Blocks" tag at the end of the name. The blocks' colors were slightly more intense in the Gaston originals, especially in the background, which was a darker shade of blue. Photo by and collection of Mark Rich. Halsam Products Co., 1960s.

Bumstead Blockhead. Fabulous flapper Blondie settled into a life of domestic bliss and comedic chaos in the comic pages of the 1940s and '50s. She then became a block-head along with her husband Dagwood. The "Blondie & Dagwood Interchangeable Blocks" were the first funny-face toys to make a splash in the early Boomer years.

Everyone in America knew the faces and expressions of these comic characters long before they appeared on a funny-face toy. "Make Dagwood and the gang laugh or cry—glare or stare!" said an advertisement at the time. Photos by and collection of Mark Rich. 5½" by 7", Gaston Mfg. Co., 1951.

comic faces of the time: Chic Young's Blondie and Dagwood, and Capitol Records' Bozo the Clown.

The general outline of "Changeable Charlie" closely resembled that of "'Ole' Million Face." Million Face went through a softening and rounding of his features from the 1930s through the 1940s. Gaston's set of blocks showed a Charlie with less distended mouth, less flamboyant bow-tie, and tidier collar. The bandages, pipe, and cigar remained options. Gaston added black eyes, lest Charlie appear too respectable, and a polka-dot shirt or pajama top.

The blocks themselves were slightly smaller, a bit lighter in color, and a bit less durable. While Schoenhut had made Million Face with lithographed cardboard sleeves to cover the wood blocks, Gaston used paper over its blocks.

Just as Schoenhut had, Gaston and its successor companies, the Charles William Doepke Manufacturing Company and Halsam Products Company, issued these toys in practical cardboard boxes.

The tray bottom of the box held the blocks neatly in place for viewing. It also made it possible to easily change the face, time and again, without removing the toy from its container. The back of the box had ten to twelve round finger holes. Pressure from a finger underneath the box lifted the desired block and eased it back down when it had been turned to its new position.

While Gaston probably had no thought of doing so when it introduced "Changeable Charlie" in 1948, the company had created one of the toys that would help cement a generation.

Unlike some of the others, such as "Slinky" or "The Game of Cootie," "Changeable Charlie" was not new. It used an old toy idea, and old toy-making materials. Yet it remained a favorite for children born through the end of the 1960s, reappearing on toy shelves year after year for over two decades.

DON'T DELAY!

"Blondie & Dagwood Interchangeable Blocks." Toy Fair for 1951 *catalog. Gaston Mfg. Co., 1951.*

BLONDIE AND DAGWOOD

While in the long run "Changeable Charlie" would prove to be a playroom standard, another Gaston funny-face toy initially showed more promise: "Blondie & Dagwood Interchangeable Blocks." Widely advertised in 1951 and available through the five-and-dimes frequented by the typical American family, the toys capitalized on the popularity of a pair of newspaper cartoon characters who had commanded public notice since the 1930s.

Unlike other make-a-face toys, the expressions possible through these block sets were familiar to almost everyone. Everyone knew Blondie's wiggle-outline hairdo, her movie-star eyebrows, and pert nose. Everyone especially knew her look of surprise at Dagwood's blundering antics. She provided beauty and a modicum of reasonable sense, in the comic strip, to contrast with Dagwood's more comical goofiness.

Comic artist Chic Young captured that comic nature perfectly in Dagwood's wooden face, with its peg-like nose, lipless mouth, dab-of-ink oval eyes, and that irrepressible pair of prominent, antenna-like cowlicks. Dagwood served as an Everyman to the American comic-reading public—an Everyman with a funny face.

Gaston's set of blocks came in "Blondie & Dagwood" pairs, and apparently also in sets featuring just Dagwood. In the larger sets, Blondie's top and back of head appeared on a single, L-shaped block. Eight other blocks

showed her forehead, ear, separate eyes, nose and cheeks, mouth and chin, neck and shoulders, and the space just in front of her face.

Ten blocks made up Dagwood's half of the set. Not only could Dagwood's expressions be changed, but various secondary characters could make entrances and exits, including boss, neighbor, kids, and dogs.

The blocks evoked the stock situations of the comic strip, since they included images of a stove with a simmering pot, Dagwood's hand carrying a "Dagwood" sandwich, and of course Dagwood's necessary comforts in life: couch and bathtub.

BOZO THE CLOWN

Much like "Changeable Charlie," the faces seen on "Bozo the Clown Changeable Blocks" were the product of pure imagination.

No real "Bozo" clown existed, beyond the jacket illustrations on records issued in the late 1940s featuring Larry Harmon's voice. Even when television sets began appearing in privileged living rooms around the country and showing images of an increasingly famous white-faced character, Bozo was a changeable clown. While he had certain made-up features that carried over from clown

Record Seller. Unlike Dagwood, whose image became famous in newspapers, Bozo's face became famous on record jackets. Photo by and collection of Mark Rich. Gaston Mfg. Co., 1950s.

The Capitol Clown. Capitol Records character, Bozo the Clown, had a more changeable, cartoon-like nature in the 1950s. Even on TV, the clown was portrayed by different actors from city to city. "Bozo the Clown Changeable Blocks" presented children with only 1,048,576 possible combinations, having only 10 pieces, in contrast to Changeable Charlie's 11. Photo by and collection of Mark Rich. 7" by 7", Gaston Mfg. Co., 1950s.

to clown, he was played by a different actor at each local television studio. Only in 1959 did a single actor in a regular TV show out of Chicago finally fix in the minds of viewers what Bozo should look and act like.

Introduced in the 1950s, Gaston's "Bozo the Clown Changeable Blocks" might have kept alive his tradition of changeability. By 1959, however, Gaston had fallen away from the toy-manufacturing scene, and the Woodworking Division of Charles William Doepke Manufacturing Company, better known for its heavy, pressed-steel toys earlier in the 1950s, had taken over Gaston's series of changeable wood toys. Doepke continued featuring the Bozo blocks that year. It was one of the last years for the toy, and perhaps the last year of the older-fashioned Bozo toys.

Yet TV won in the end. Toys based on the idea of an imaginary clown, rather than on a particular TV clown, were consigned to the island of played-out and worn-out toy ideas. By 1960, one of the biggest names in the wood-toy business, Halsam Products Company of Chicago, had taken over the line of changeable blocks from Doepke. The big clown toy of that year, helped toward success by the new popularity of Bob Bell as the clown on the WGN-TV's "Bozo Show," was a large floppy doll: "Bozo, the Capitol Clown," a vinyl-faced rag and flannel figure by Renall Dolls.

The Bozo changeable make-a-face toy disappeared from toy shelves.

The clowns of real life had long capitalized on the funny-face idea. In fact, the concept of the clown and the concept of the funny face must have arisen together. How odd, then, that when funny-face toys came into their own in the 1950s, relatively few toys used the clown as the jumping-off point.

Maybe human faces in their natural, or naturally unnatural, state were simply funnier than clown faces.

Or maybe toy manufacturers realized clown faces did indeed seem funny to kids, but usually funny in one way only. Bozo, for instance, always had to have a big, red, round nose. One of the biggest sources for playful humor in a funny-face toy was the nose. As opposed to the seemingly infinite shape possibilities of the regular, fleshly nose, Bozo's nose was one shape, and one shape only. His eyebrows were always the same high arches. His hair always had to be the same flaming red mass full of unruly strands. The top of his head always had to be bald.

You might have thought a funny-face toy based on a more generic clown, with more changeable noses and eyebrows and hair, would have been the success of the 1950s. Yet "Bozo the Clown Changeable Blocks" appear to have been the top make-a-clown-face toy of the times.

Typical clown toys of the times could be found, for instance, inside the "Blue Bird Circus Wagon," made by the National Latex Products Company of Ashland, Ohio, in the mid-1950s. This wagon-shaped cardboard box contained colorful balloons. Some had pictures of circus animals on them. Others were odd-shaped, having bulbous protuberances for noses and clown faces printed around those long snouts. The clown faces made children laugh because of their association with the circus and comic routines. They suggested unicycles and tiny parasols and pratfalls.

Other popular clown toys suggested the same thing. The inflatable bop-bag "Bobo the Clown" by Doughboy Industries of New Richmond, Wisconsin, with its round, red, punch-able nose, or the plastic clown-headed roly-polys by Gerber Plastics Company, used clown faces to keep the children smiling. The faces hardly needed to change, or be changeable, to be funny.

Bozo was a double whammy celebrity in the 1950s, appearing on records, and thus on popular radio, and also on local TV stations across the country. Toy manufacturers were quickly learning the value of linking toys to television presences, especially after the 1954 and 1955 Disney triumph of its "Davy Crockett" episodes, ABC-TV's *Disneyland*, and the 1955 success of the *Mickey Mouse Club* TV show.

Even if Gaston had produced a more inventive changeable clown toy—which it may well have done, somewhere along the line—in all likelihood, Bozo the Clown still would have been left sitting at the top of the block-head heap.

Better Than Charlie. *When Halsam took over the "Changeable" blocks line, it introduced a funny-face block set even a little crazier than its most famous funny face. Her name was "Changeable Charlie's Aunt." A true fashion leader, she kept an egg-filled bird's nest, purple propeller-bearing cap, and a goldfish bowl among her headpiece options. She could look aging and matronly, weirdly stylish and pouty, or even goofily pugilistic, with a boxing glove visible below. Ribbons, bows, pins, and combs gave the toy more extreme variations. Photos by and collection of Mark Rich. 5½" by 7", Halsam Products Co., 1960s.*

Vegetable Space People. *An apple-headed robot confronts the universe, while other robots of the 1950s look on from the distance.*

Pressman's "Space Faces" was the only funny-face toy of the early postwar years to build upon children's fascination with outer space and the far future. While the kit's various "facial" features could be mixed and matched, they could also be used to assemble two distinct figures. One was a robot. The other was a strange alien.

Hassenfeld Bros. missed the boat, or rather the rocket, in letting another company take potato-heads into space. The Hasbro line would have no space spuds until the late 1960s, fifteen years after Pressman's "Space Faces" took the initiative. Collection of Jeff Potocsnak; photo by Mark Rich. Pressman Toy Corp., 1953.

CHAPTER 3

WHAT WAS IT ABOUT 1953?

*Sure, a few kids before the War sported Buck Rogers Rocket Pistols,
running around the neighborhood and blasting all the aliens
and bad guys to smithereens.
In 1953, however, kids launched into a Space Craze that would
make the later Space Race look dismally tame in comparison.
They created imaginative scenarios with colorful plastic space people,
donned fish-bowl helmets, and graduated from blasters to
massive atomic disintegrators.
Even the vegetable bin tried to escape Earth's gravity.
Meanwhile, on Earth, other spud-like toys flew off
store shelves into children's hands.*

Funny-face toys enjoyed a top year in 1953. Not only did Hassenfeld Brothers greatly increase its line to include new characters—Mrs. Potato Head, Spud, and Yam—but competitors sprang from the woodwork. Hassenfeld Brothers apparently made an effort to protect its trade name, as indicated by Pressman Toy Corporation's backing away from "Potato Faces" as the name for its new funny-face kit. Yet the Rhode Island firm could do nothing to stop the many almost-but-not-quite-the-same toys from appearing on the market and winning their own share of American children's affections.

Undoubtedly the best of the competition came from Pressman, which issued the toy that took vegetables where no animal could go—into outer space, one of the greatest staging areas for the imaginations of 1950s children.

"Space Faces" excelled as a toy in many ways. Pressman obviously had its corporate finger on the pulse of the times. When "Space Faces" was released in 1953, the kit appeared alongside a rash of other space-toy hits—the incredibly popular "Space People" plastic play-set figures and vehicles from Archer Plastics of Bronx, New York; the space-gothic repeating cap pistol "Atomic Disintegrator" by the Hubley Manufacturing Company of Lancaster,

Pennyslvania; and the breathtaking "Streamline Dream Car," an atypical toy by musical-toy maker Mattel of Los Angeles, California.

"Space Faces" kits emphasized as many non-potato fruits and vegetables as possible. On the

Asteroid Detector Eyebrows. This futuristic figure is nearly complete, missing only the spring extensions of its arms. In the photos of the robot and alien, the spring from inside a ball-point pen serves for one arm. Collection of Jeff Potocsnak; photo by Mark Rich. Detail of box, "Space Faces," Pressman Toy Corp., 1953.

Fruitful Futures. *"Space Faces" fed the imaginations of children already inspired by such extravaganzas as DuMont's "Captain Video," a television show with cardboard sets and a budget smaller than Pressman must have had for making its toy.*

Imaginatively packaged, the kit ranked among the most elaborately designed space toys of the time. Even the lettering on the box evoked the riveted metal of a spaceship or robot. The interior of the box, shown here, shows a high degree of both imagination and care in its design and execution. Photo by Mark Rich. Collection of Jeff Potocsnak. Pressman Toy Corp., 1953.

"Space Faces." *In its packaging, Pressman emphasized non-potatoes for use as heads. On the box top, an imposing, orange-headed robot commands the landscape. The one potato-headed alien, in contrast, is the smallest character to be seen, at farthest left, directly in front of the orange space ship. Pressman's box was distinct in featuring a full landscape—in this case, a barren planet-scape with a streamlined craft shooting through the blue space above. Collection of Jeff Potocsnak. 8" by 13", Pressman Toy Corp., 1953.*

box top, an orange-headed creature took the limelight. Inside, the facial pieces were held in place by a foam head, just as in "Mr. Potato Head" kits. In this case, however, the head was round, and was placed in front of a suggestively orange circle. Around the edges of the box, illustrations showed more vegetable possibilities than did any Hassenfeld boxes or instruction sheets. Carrot, green pepper, apple, beet, pear, potato, tomato, lemon, cucumber, and onion all showed up around the sides, in outer space and robotic guises.

The kits also managed to keep their distance from "Mr. Potato Head" kits by being clearly different in focus, and clearly imaginative in approach. No simple eyes, noses, mouths, ears, eyebrows, and hats appeared here.

The "exciting new vegetable space toy with supersonic ACTION parts" had no mere eyes, but Super Sight Eyes. It wore no mere hat, but the beehive-shaped Cyclotron Headpiece. Or it could wear a propeller-like Sonic Resonator Headpiece, or the Tele-Radar Helmet Disc. It could sport a bizarre, red, fanged mouth, or a green, grille-like Robot Mouth.

Rather than ears, it had Sound Stabilizer Earpieces; instead of a nose, the Fission Control Nosepiece, Cosmic Ray Nosepiece, or Electronic Ray Nosepiece. Its eyebrows were not black flannel cutouts, but Asteroid Detector Eyebrows of shiny red plastic.

Its green, barrel-shaped, robotic body had no special name. Nor did its spiky, splayed-finger hands, which were intended to be stretched out at the end of springs. Nor did its springy antennae. For feet, it had either boxlike red clompers, to fit below the robot's tin-can body, or clawed Anti-Gravity Feet to match the fanged mouth.

Besides its timeliness, the "Space Faces" kit had many things going for it: brightly colorful pieces to contrast with the flesh-tones of the Potato Head pieces; imaginative, Deco-influenced design ideas; and a box with a fun scene on the front, in contrast to the plain-jane "Mr. Potato Head" boxes simply showing the figures.

It was literally the Face of the Future.

Or rather the Funny Face of the Future.

■ ■ ■

A SPACE VEGETABLE NATURALLY NEEDED AN ELECTRONIC RAY NOSEPIECE!

■ ■ ■

Robot. Photo by Mark Rich.

MISTER FUNNY FACE

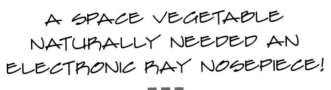

Jack Pressman & Co. established itself in the 1920s and 1930s with an extensive and diverse line of playthings, including spinning tops, bubble outfits, jackstones, toy telephones, ten pins, games, table tennis, table croquet, and science sets.

It also issued such home-making toys as toy sewing machines and knitting sets.

The firm became Pressman Toy Corporation after World War II. Meanwhile it found its niche in the toy world, expanding to include doctor bags, nurse kits, and art sets. In other words, Pressman had established a line of toys much like the one Hassenfeld Brothers was establishing during the war, and it occupied a place in the industry much like the one the Rhode Island firm wanted to occupy.

It probably seemed only fitting that when the Hassenfelds branched out into "Mr. Potato Head" kits, Pressman should then return the favor of horning-in on established territory and introduce its "Space Faces" kits.

Another firm had a remarkably similar profile in the 1950s. Peerless Playthings Company of Ridgefield Park, New Jersey, was developing a line featuring toy guns, table tennis, and games, as well as toy jewelry, crayon sets, coloring sets, clay sets, and doctor and nurse kits.

Alien. The second figure to be made with the set was more clearly an alien or monster figure, with fangs and pointed ears. All pieces in the box, however, were given imaginary high-tech names. Photo by Mark Rich.

Almost Better than the Original. *The pieces of "Mister Funny Face" looked remarkably like Mr. Potato Head's. The eyes, seen here with other features on the board in which they came packed, were ever so slightly different. So was the body, which was more detailed and interesting than Mr. Potato Head's. Collection of Jeff Potocsnak; photo by Mark Rich. Peerless Playthings Co., 1953.*

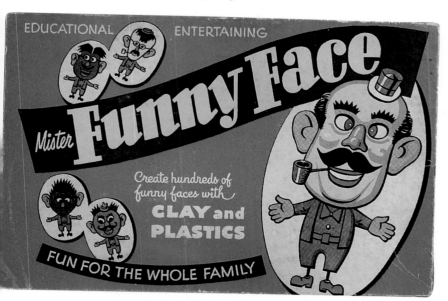

Mr. Clay Face. *In its take-off on the Potato Head idea, the "Mister Funny Face" kit recommended using endlessly malleable clay or plasticene for the head, not vegetables. It still came packed with a convenient foam head. Collection of Jeff Potocsnak. 8½" by 13", Peerless Playthings Co., 1953.*

Could it have happened otherwise than it, too, should quickly devise a competitor to the "Mr. Potato Head" kits?

Its entry in this growing toy-making arena was "Mister Funny Face." On the cover appeared a large, yellow-faced character with a pipe in his mouth. He had a hat, eyebrows, mustache, nose, crossed eyes, and smiling, white-centered mouth. The pipe, true enough, came out the right side of his mouth, while Mr. Potato Head seemed always depicted with pipe on the left. He looked distinctly potato-like.

However, he was not a potato at all. As the side of the box explained, "Young and old will have fun creating hundreds of funny faces with CLAY and PLASTICS." In other words, a ball of clay was to receive the pointed spikes of noses, eyes, and mouths.

The pieces looked closely similar, but not exactly like, Mr. Potato Head's pieces. The large, round eyes had bull's-eye centers. They and the other plastic eyes had black centers, not blue. The noses looked a bit different. The hats were a bit smaller and offered a distinct range of types: a top hat, a fedora, and an oval derby. The hands were molded on only one side, not two. The glasses were a little thicker, with a nose piece only slightly rounded.

Several pieces seemed superior to the original. The feet, for instance, were detailed and actually looked like shoes. The body was nicely detailed with jacket, buttoned shirt, bow tie, and belt. The limbs curved gently, instead of sticking straight out like sticks.

Many of Mr. Potato Head's features seemed smooth, featureless, and boring in comparison.

As an added bonus, the playing child found a beard among the felt hair-pieces, a bit of facial furriness unknown in the Mr. Potato Head universe.

THE QUICK-CHANGE TOY

Perhaps the oddest of 1950s funny-face toys was "Juggle-Head," first issued in 1953.

It, too, had a decidedly potato-like look. Unlike "Mr. Potato Head," "Space Faces," "Mister Funny-Face," or some other sets of the time, "Juggle-Head" provided a fixed-shape, three-dimensional head. Made of a cardboard shell, the basic head was also somewhat peanut-shaped, with a smaller top half for the forehead, and a wider, rounded bottom half depicting a generous chin and cheeks. The flesh-toned head itself came already decorated—spots and dashes were painted on for eyes, nose, mouth, and brows; and the cheeks were nicely rouged. Underneath these spots, and on the sides of the head, however, the manufacturer had planted magnets.

Made by Langwood Products of New York City, and later of Brooklyn, the "Juggle-Head" kit introduced a new element to the funny-face field. Not only did it have normal pieces for making human faces, it also included snouts, beaks, and muzzles for creating pigs, dogs, and ducks, or some combination thereof. The accessories, made of pressed wood or a composition-like substance, each had a small metal plate attached to the back. These could be placed against the head, to be held there magnetically.

The toys had a rough look, since the head and pieces lacked the polished smoothness and sheen of plastic. Even so, the toy had a kind of bizarre charm—and sometimes even an uncanny spookiness.

Langwood soon came out with "Juggle-Head Junior." A smaller kit, it centered around a smaller, pear-shaped head with molded-on eyes and eyebrows. The head contained magnets only for nose, mouth, and ears. Although fewer in number, the accessories did include a new, chicken-like beak. They also included the unusual features of hats made of paper, apparently intended to be held in place by the playing child.

"Juggle-Head" may have been the first magnetic funny-face toy of its kind; or it may have appeared roughly simultaneously with "Magnetic Comic Faces," or some early version

Animal Changeability. While unmistakably potato-like in shape and outline, "Juggle-Head" kits took a decidedly non-vegetable approach. Metal plates hold facial features to the unchangeable head, which has magnets inside. "Juggle-Head" kits also introduced animal features, which increased the fanciful possibilities of the toy. This close-up of the box-top shows children running with animal features in their arms. The strangeness of this picture reflects, in some degree, the strangeness of the toy itself. Collection of Jeff Potocsnak; photo by Mark Rich. 9" by 13" box, Langwood Products, 1953.

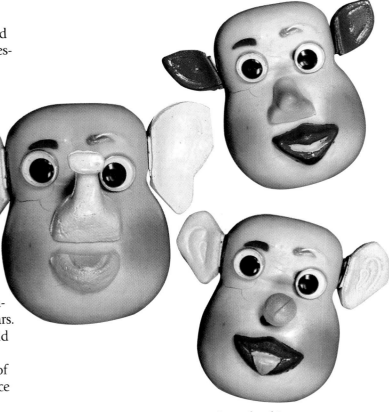

Juggle-Heads. Probably no other funny-face kit was quite as bizarre and unsettling as Juggle-Head. Langwood's toy did easily what Mr. Potato Head could not do well: be spooky. Photos by Mark Rich.

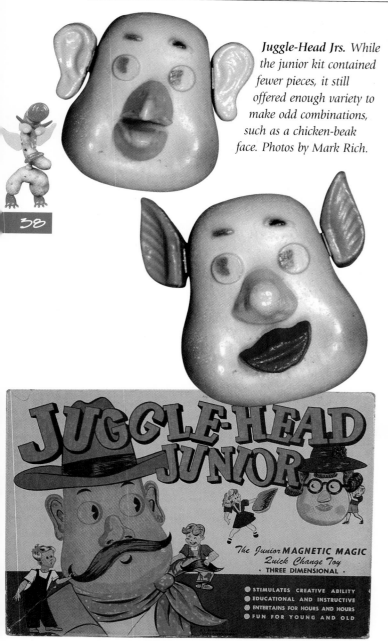

Juggle-Head Jrs. While the junior kit contained fewer pieces, it still offered enough variety to make odd combinations, such as a chicken-beak face. Photos by Mark Rich.

Junior Magnet-Face. The "Juggle-Head Junior" kit contained only nine accessory pieces for its face. Having the eyes fixed to the face, however, did not greatly limit the possibilities. The original "Juggle Head" kits had only one kind of eye to attach in the first place. Juggle-Head Junior's head measured 3½" tall, against Juggle-Head's 4" head. Collection of Jeff Potocsnak. 9" by 13", Langwood Products, 1950s.

of "Magnetic Funny Faces." Whether first or not, for a brief time the toy enjoyed wide circulation, spreading across the States through the pages of department store catalogs.

FRONTIER FACES

Looking back, it comes as something of a surprise that more funny-face toys did not take off where "Space Faces" left off.

Public fascination with the future was steadily growing, as was being reflected all over: in the appearance of advertisements in popular magazines that took future life on the Moon or in Outer Space for granted; in the appearance of such well-crafted and well-received movies as *The Day the Earth Stood Still* in 1951 and *War of the Worlds* in 1953; and in the dynamic growth of the science fiction magazine field, in which a few writers, including Cyril Kornbluth, William Tenn, Kurt Vonnegut, Judith Merril, and Fritz Leiber, were raising pulp writing to the level of serious literature.

Kids, too, were thrilled by the idea of the future, and they did their part to make futuristic toys hits through the end of the '50s. Even late in the decade, when Westerns were even more the rage than they had been in the 1940s and earlier 1950s, spaceships kept zooming and robots kept trundling around their separate galleries of the toy-manufacturing world.

Yet somehow funny-face toy manufacturers let the early Space Age slide by almost unnoticed. Was it that Outer Space was not intrinsically funny? Were the faces behind the clear panes of

Cardboard Clowns. The five large clown faces in this set were printed on board. The features are removable, in the manner of a tray puzzle. Collection of Jeff Potocsnak. "Funny Face," Whitman Publishing Co., 1950s or '60s.

helmets too serious?

The fact that toy manufacturers made no Western funny-face toys, even during that Western hey-day of the late 1950s, suggests an answer. Perhaps the notion of the Frontier was still too important to citizens of the States, who still considered their nation young. That notion of the Frontier's importance was shared by their children, whose grim-faced plastic cowboys chased grim-faced plastic Indians across the living room floor.

The Frontier was too inimical and uncongenial to the light-heartedness and joy suggested by the funny-face toy. That toy's proper province lay within the comfort of a settled, established society, and within the comfort of a settled, established home. Had Pressman only realized this, the firm might have introduced a Mrs. Space Face, and thus have given the Space Face clan a more permanent place in the playroom toy box.

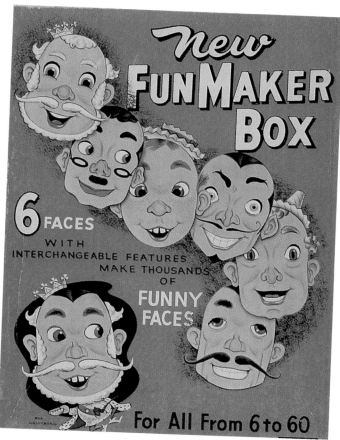

New Funmaker. Some funny-face toys were suited to children too young to be given a "Mr. Potato Head" kit. One such toy was this "New Funmaker Box," which featured "six faces with interchangeable features." Collection of Jeff Potocsnak. The Saalfield Publishing Co., 1950s or 1960s.

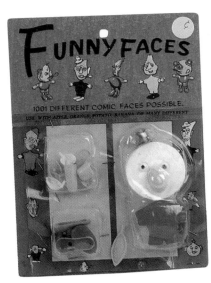

Funny Faces. The Potato Head idea sometimes appeared in blatant rip-off versions, as in this kit, probably issued in the 1950s. As in the Hassenfeld original, the kit supplied a foam head inside. The plastic features were made from a cheaper, softer plastic. Collection of Jeff Potocsnak. "Funny Faces," unknown manufacturer, 1950s.

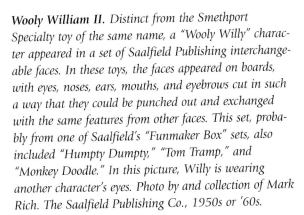

Wooly William II. Distinct from the Smethport Specialty toy of the same name, a "Wooly Willy" character appeared in a set of Saalfield Publishing interchangeable faces. In these toys, the faces appeared on boards, with eyes, noses, ears, mouths, and eyebrows cut in such a way that they could be punched out and exchanged with the same features from other faces. This set, probably from one of Saalfield's "Funmaker Box" sets, also included "Humpty Dumpty," "Tom Tramp," and "Monkey Doodle." In this picture, Willy is wearing another character's eyes. Photo by and collection of Mark Rich. The Saalfield Publishing Co., 1950s or '60s.

Sheer Vegetable Beauty. *Mrs. Potato Head enlarged the possibilities of the Potato Head toys, adding numerous new parts to make it possible for children to create female characters. The eyebrows made from a printed plastic sheet, the half-moon eyes, the mouth with white center, and the cardboard hat brim are all characteristic of original, older sets. Photo by Mark Rich.*

CHAPTER 4

FIRST CAME MR. POTATO HEAD.

Then his vegetable wife.
"Fascinating individual! As sweet as a yam—
tough as a turnip, or comical as a carrot …
Complete feminine accessories, including a wig of real hair!"

If Mr. Potato Head was a domestic being,
he needed a full household:
Wife and kids—and pets.

41

While Mr. Potato Head was not a household name in 1952, by 1953 the toy had entered literally millions of households—if not as an actual toy, than as a cheerful and amusing image seen by every member of the family. All they had to do was sit down with an issue of *Look*, *Life*, or *Good Housekeeping*—or sit down in front of the TV. Through the power of an enormous advertising fund, Mr. Potato Head became almost as well known as the TV figures his advertisements supported.

In new ads appearing across the nation, however, Mr. Potato Head was not appearing alone. He was no longer a solitary, one-of-a-kind toy.

The creative minds at Hassenfeld Brothers rightly perceived that Mr. Potato Head, as a representative American Everyman, needed company. If he was to represent a figure stepping out of everyday life, he needed other everyday figures around him. At a time when the nation's image of the happy American family was being adroitly molded and reshaped by advertisements and television serials into a thing of almost unattainable perfection, it struck Hassenfeld Brothers that Mr. Potato Head required a Mrs.

Fittingly, she made her debut not as a solitary toy but as part of a set. Combination kits offered the pieces for making Mr. and Mrs. Potato Head together. She also appeared in full-family sets, together with "brother Spud and sister Yam." Despite the entry of the kids, Mrs. Potato Head was the true innovation in the line.

Mr. and Mrs. POTATO HEAD
the joyful toy of 1001 faces!

Hasbro Toys are truly inspirational — and there are none finer!
Designed for maximum educational play value,
a Hasbro Toy is a toy with a purpose.

Meet the Missus! Flush with its 1952 success, Hassenfeld Bros. began enlarging the Potato Head family the next year, introducing Mrs. Potato Head and two Potato Head children. While promoting these toys heavily, the Rhode Island company continued to largely focus its energies on craft, educational, and make-believe toys and play sets, including doctor and nurse kits, "Beaux Arts" paint sets, "Hobby Craft" paint-by-number sets, "Junior Miss" cosmetic sets and sewing kits, "Let's Play" activity sets, "Jolly Hobby" finger paints, and "Teach-A-Toy" craft and educational sets. Hassenfeld Bros. advertisement, Life, 1953.

King and Queen. When the "Funny Face Combination Kit" introduced the second most famous potato personality, Hassenfeld Bros. called them the "King and Queen of Laughs." Note the black-and-white images of the figures on the box. A deluxe kit, it sold for the deluxe price of $2. Collection of Jeff Potocsnak. 10" by 13½", Hassenfeld Bros., 1953.

Adding Life. Once it began the heavy advertising campaign that turned the Potato Heads into toy superstars, Hassenfeld Bros. added color to the boxes, as well as the all-important mention of America's most popular magazine of the 1940s and '50s. Collection of Jeff Potocsnak. 10" by 13½", Hassenfeld Bros., later 1953 and '54.

With her, a whole new set of accessories arrived. They instantly changed and made complete the Potato Head world. Because of her, Potato Head kits were the best both-sexes toys of the time, and perhaps of the entire Baby Boom period. While girls willingly played with "Mr. Potato Head" kits in 1952, and still did so in 1953, now they enjoyed expanded options. They had two characters to build: a funny-face man and a funny-face woman. Girls undoubtedly role-played with the character that the first kit produced. Now their role-playing could expand to include essentially the whole cast of the typical domestic stage.

Mrs. Potato Head's presence added a new body, new feet, new facial features, and new accessories to the Potato Head kits. Her body showed she was clearly a mature, busty woman. She wore a short skirt, showing more of her legs than Mr. Potato Head's pants did. Her shoes had low heels, with pretty bows. New facial features added the possibilities of prettier eyebrows and more feminine mouths. She had a flowing luxuriance of reddish-brown hair. She sported fancy hats with scalloped cardboard brims.

Her instruction sheet echoed her husband's:

"An introduction to Mrs. Potato Head—the most wonderful little friend a boy or girl ever had," it said. "You'll enjoy making these very funny characters, and it's all so simple. Just stick a real, live potato on her plastic body. Then select a set of eyes, a nose, a pair of lips, ears, hair wig, hat and there you are!"

The children, who never came packaged alone, were essentially the same as Mr. and Mrs. Potato Head. Their only differences of appearance were the smaller foam heads they came with.

Perhaps Hassenfeld Brothers did this as a way of suggesting to children that they simply find smaller potatoes for making the small-fries.

■ ■ ■

"Let the skie raine potatoes." —Shakespeare,
"The Merry Wives of Windsor"

■ ■ ■

Advertised in Life. *As the 1950s progressed, the Potato Head family continued their prominence in the Hassenfeld line, being the central figure of promotions and advertising in the* New York Times, Good Housekeeping, Parents' Magazine, *and* Saturday Evening Post. *Nothing spoke louder to the toy industry, and to the world, of Hassenfeld's crowning success, however, than its continuing promotions through the massively popular* Life.

In this quartet of Potato Head sandwich-board figures, Mrs. Potato Head wears the Life *placard, while the Onion Head wears the seal of commendation from the Consumer Service Bureau of* Parents' Magazine. *Hassenfeld Bros. catalog, 1956.*

His House. *In his second year, Mr. Potato Head appeared in an attractive new window box, shaped like a small house. Collection of Jeff Potocsnak. 9" by 9", Hassenfeld Bros., 1953.*

Santa's Vehicle. *With its popularity soaring during and after World War II,* Life *magazine commanded the attention of the nation, much as major TV networks would in later years.* Life, *a family magazine, became the vehicle for the most ambitious national toy promotions as each successive Christmas approached. The first toy manufacturer to launch a postwar campaign in its pages may have been the Lionel Corp. Other major advertisers included Charles William Doepke Manufacturing Company and Fleischaker & Baum.* Life *subscription inset, Dec. 3, 1945. Photo by Mark Rich.*

Her House. *The new window boxes for the Potato Heads would remain standard for several years. After their first year, the boast "As Advertised in* Life*" appeared on the house's roof. Collection of Jeff Potocsnak. 9" by 9", "Mrs. Potato Head," Hassenfeld Bros., 1953.*

1

2 Walt Disney's Disneyland Pencil Case

WALT DISNEY MICKEY MOUSE PENCIL CASE

A TRADITION OF SCHOOL COMPANIONS

In addition to moving deeper into the toy world with art and craft sets, Hassenfeld Brothers was venturing into the world of licensed characters.

By the 1950s, the firm was enjoying a working relationship with Walt Disney Productions, and was letting Mickey Mouse, Donald Duck, and Pluto sell its three main sizes of traditional cardboard pencil boxes.

The simplest and smallest was the "slide box" design, measuring a bit over eight inches long and consisting of a cardboard sleeve with a shallow tray that slid inside. A full-color print featuring the characters was printed separately, and glued on top.

The next larger size was a nine-inch long snap-shut case with two compartments. Beneath the snap-down lid was one tray, for rulers and other school items. Below that was a single pull-drawer for more supplies. The deluxe version was similar, but larger, measuring eleven inches long. It featured two pull-drawers beneath the top tray.

The company did have the sense to capitalize on its own licensed characters, too, even if for only a few years. By the mid-1950s, the Potato Head family, including Yam and Spud, appeared on the three sizes of traditional pencil boxes. Other kinds of pencil containers, such as the vinyl pencil pouches and vinyl school bags, seemed to remain the province of the immensely popular Disney characters.

In the first few years after the introduction of its funny-face kits, it appeared Mr. Potato Head might become the trademark figure for the entire Hasbro toy line. However, Hasbro tended to favor the rising stars of TV, whether from the "Captain Kangaroo," "Leave It To Beaver," or "Disneyland" shows.

Nothing reflected this more strongly than Mr. Potato Head's disappearance from the tops of Hassenfeld Brothers' pencil boxes, after 1955.

7 Walt Disney's DISNEYLAND OIL PAINTING by Numbers — HASSENFELD BROS., INC. PAWTUCKET, R.I.

8

6

❶ Off to School with Mickey. *Hassenfeld Brothers discovered two keys to selling success in the pencil-box field: first, fill the boxes; second, decorate them, acquiring the rights to put licensed characters on the top if possible. The Disney characters of Pluto, Mickey, and Donald appeared on Hasbro pencil boxes until the Disneyland design took its place, probably in later 1955. Some unlicensed boxes included generic safety and "Jr. Rodeo" themes or bore the Francis Bacon motto that seems to have been adopted by the company for its educational items: "Knowledge is power."*

Despite its age, the box shown still contains eleven multi-colored crayons, marked "Made in U.S.A.," a ruler, a small, rectangular and now quite hard eraser, and three pencils. The box may be an earlier example of its kind, since the pencils are by Eagle Pencil Co. of New York City, rather than being Hassenfeld's own Empire or Pedigree pencils. Collection of and photo by Mark Rich. Roughly 8" by 4½", "Walt Disney Mickey Mouse Pencil Case," Hassenfeld Bros., possibly as early as the 1940s through mid-'50s.

❷ Casey Jr. Pencils. *Tinkerbell and Mickey Mouse arrive with a trainload of pencils. Collection of and photo by Mark Rich. Roughly 8" by 4", "Walt Disney's Disneyland Pencil Case," Hassenfeld Bros., mid 1950s to early '60s.*

❸ Space Ship. *Pencil cases appeared in a variety of imaginative forms, including jackknives, trophies, large pencils, and space-age rockets. One example is the mid-1950s "Rocket Pencil Case" in "brilliant Metolite finish," with ruler, pencils, and built-in pencil sharpener. By 1956 the firm was using the space ship to promote Disneyland. "Disneyland Rocket Pencil Case," Hassenfeld Bros. catalog, later 1950s.*

❹ "Soldier Crayon Case." *Hassenfeld Bros. catalog, mid-1950s.*

❺ Deluxe Double-Drawer. *The Potato Head family appeared on three kinds of boxes: the "slide box style pencil case"; the "snap button drawer style box," with one pull-out drawer for extra supplies; and the "deluxe double drawer pencil case," which had two pull-out drawers. Photo by and collection of Mark Rich. 5" by 11" by 2", "School Days Potato Head Pencil Case," Hassenfeld Bros., about 1953–55.*

❻ "Adding Machine Pouch." *Hassenfeld Bros. catalog, mid-1950s.*

❼ Paint-By-Numberland. *One of the biggest events of the decade was the opening of Disneyland in 1955. Hassenfeld Bros. immediately leapt on the bandwagon. Among its offerings were its "Disneyland Oil Paint-By-Numbers" sets, available in Fantasyland, Frontierland, Tomorrowland, and Adventureland sets, selling for a dollar apiece. Hassenfeld Bros. catalog, 1955.*

❽ Crayon Companions. *The introduction of hard plastic to Hassenfeld manufacturing options led to such attractive "school companions" as this "Clown Crayon Case," sold with six colored crayons inside. Hassenfeld Bros. catalog, mid-1950s.*

❸

❹

❺

SCHOOL DAYS POTATO HEAD PENCIL CASE

46

Photo by Mark Rich.

❸ **Pipe Dreams.** *The "Loony-Kins" combined Mickey Mouse Club comic figures with body features similar to Potato Head bodies. Unlike the Potato Head kits, however, children assembled these body pieces by means of connecting "fuzzy wires" or pipe cleaners. The figures could be set on a plastic stage, with a cardboard shack providing the backdrop. The play sets proved a hit in their first season. Collection of Jeff Potocsnak. 15½" by 11½", Hassenfeld Bros., 1956 and later '50s.*

Junior Miss House.
In the mid-1950s, Hassenfeld Brothers used the Mr. Potato Head house box concept for a sewing kit in the "Junior Miss" line. Hassenfeld Bros. catalog, 1956.

Junior Miss. *In the 1950s, Hasbro issued a variety of activity and make-believe toys for girls under the "Junior Miss" name, including this vinyl cosmetics kit, measuring 9" long by almost 5" tall. The kit was issued with a cardboard insert that held a pink plastic hand mirror, comb, and compact, along with other make-up items.*

Other Junior Miss items fell along traditional lines: cosmetic kits, cases, purses, and travel bags; sewing kits and baskets; trousseau sets that included dolls and pre-cut wardrobe pieces ready to be sewn together; knitting sets; and embroidery cases and sets. At least one early set appeared in a cardboard window box styled as a small house, much like the boxes for Mr. Potato Head sets of the time. A "Junior Miss Boudoir Vanity" came out in 1956.

Craft sets for slightly older girls, including embroidery sets, appeared under the "Jolly Hobby" name in the early to mid-'50s. By 1960 Hasbro introduced the "Deb-U-Teen" cosmetic sets and cases for increasingly style-conscious Boomer teens.

Photos by and collection of Mark Rich. "Junior Miss Make-Up Kit," late '50s to early '60s, Hassenfeld Bros, Inc.

Side Order of Fries. *The biggest set of Mr. Potato Head's second year introduced the small fries, named Spud and Yam. While they appeared smaller on the box, the only parts smaller or different in the new kids were the foam heads, 2" tall instead of the 2½" of their parents' heads. Collection of Jeff Potocsnak. 12" by 17", "Mr. and Mrs. Potato Head," Hassenfeld Bros., 1953.*

Over 100 Pieces. *As with the smaller Mr. and Mrs. Potato Head set, the deluxe kit went from black and white to color after heavier advertising started. Collection of Jeff Potocsnak. 12" by 17", "Mr. and Mrs. Potato Head," Hassenfeld Bros., later 1953 and '54.*

Circus Wagon. *After Mr. and Mrs. Potato Head appeared in house-shaped window boxes in 1953, it was fitting that the Potato Head animals should appear in similar but distinctive window boxes. Collection of Jeff Potocsnak. 9" x 9", "Spud-Ettes," Hassenfeld Bros., late 1953 or '54.*

48

FROM DOCTOR BAGS TO HEADER BAGS

Professor Potato. Mr. Potato Head helped promote Hasbro's standard line in the 1950s, including its pencil cases. Hassenfeld Bros. catalog, 1955.

An important niche in the postwar toy world was the manufacturing of "rack" items, sometimes called "self-service" or counter items.

These tended to be inexpensive assortments of toys, craft supplies, and games, usually packaged in "header bags," which were plastic bags with a cardboard "header" at the top. Sometimes, for stiffening the package, cardboard backing was inserted within the bag. The new "blister" card, with a stiffer transparent plastic holding the toys against the backer card, was a new option for rack items in the 1950s.

In whatever form, rack items were designed to hang on hooks. Usually the manufacturers supplied pegboards, metal racks, or spinner racks to the retailers, to make it as easy as possible for stores to stock and then re-stock their products.

Hassenfeld Brothers issued a variety of familiar kits in its "self-service, year-round toys" rack selections, ranging from "Let's Play School," "Dolly Nurse," "Junior Doctor," and "Dainty Miss Cosmetic" kits, to packages of plastic cowboy figures, or the "Mischief Kit," containing simple and harmless trick items.

The Potato Heads seemed slow to move into these cheaper lodgings, doing so in later 1955 and '56. Surprisingly, the "Spud-Ettes," usually spelled "Spudettes" on header bags, were the first to make the transition. While the new Potato Head and "Captain Kangaroo's Pets" featured new styles of plastic animal bodies for the Spud-Ettes, the first rack version still used the original Potato Head human body.

"Create 1,001 human-like animals with ordinary fruits or vegetables," the firm's advertising promised.

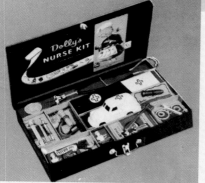

Junior Doctor. Kits by Hassenfeld Bros. for playing hospital helped the company move more deeply into toy manufacturing during World War II. They continued to hold an important place in the Hasbro line afterwards. This clear-sided vinyl "Junior Doctor Bag," introduced in 1955, held eighteen toy medical items and sold for $2. Many of the doctor and nurse kits included toy plastic ambulances, as does the nurse kit seen to the left. Hassenfeld Bros. catalog, 1955.

"Dolly's Nurse Kit." Hassenfeld Bros. catalog, 1955.

"Mr Potato Head." Inexpensive rack versions of Potato Head kits helped Hasbro compete against cheap copycat kits. Collection of Jeff Potocsnak. Hassenfeld Bros., later 1950s.

Pla-Pak. The self-service "Pla-Paks" at the end of the 1950s and early '60s appeared in window boxes. Collection of Jeff Potocsnak. "Spudettes," Hassenfeld Bros., probably late 1950s.

Comic Animal Pets. In the 1950s Hasbro kits appeared in countless five-and-dimes as rack items. This "Spudettes" was among the first of the Potato Head rack packages, selling for 59 cents. Collection of Jeff Potocsnak. Hassenfeld Bros., 1955–56.

Comic Animal Pets. Blister cards began to be more common in dime stores in the 1960s, although the display method never entirely supplanted the earlier method of using polyethylene bags. Collection of Jeff Potocsnak. "Spudettes," Hassenfeld Bros., probably early 1960s.

WINDOW-BOX SHOPPING

In 1953, Hassenfeld's individual Potato Head sets were still being issued in dollar kits. Now, however, they came in attractive cardboard boxes with acetate window fronts.

Literally windows, these gave full-length views of either the Mr. or the Mrs. standing in the door of the cardboard house, which came with a convenient carrying handle at the top.

From windows to each side of the door, additional facial pieces peered. Mr. Potato Head came in a yellow "house"; Mrs. Potato Head came in a red one. Above the door of these twenty-eight-piece sets appeared the continuing promise: "Any fruit or vegetable makes a funny face."

In 1953, window boxes with clear acetate viewing panes were still a relatively new marketing device. A few other companies experimented with this packaging, including Renwal Toy Corporation, with its various "Jolly Twins" assortments of doll house furniture and figures; A. C. Gilbert, with its "Gilbert Mysto Magic" and "Gilbert Puzzle Set" assortments; American Metal Specialties Corp. with its "Doll-E-Feedette" and other doll accessory assortments; Ohio Art Company, with its "Plastic Farm Animals" and similar sets; and Tee-Vee Toys with its "Howdy Doody Plastic Toys." Within a few years, such packaging would become so ubiquitous that shoppers would forget those times when items often had to be bought sight-unseen.

Hassenfeld Brothers remained aggressive in developing the Potato Head line. By the end of 1953, or early the next year, it had expanded the Potato Head domestic scene by the last necessary step by adding the family pets.

Among the most fanciful of the early Potato Head toys, the "Spud-Ettes" were initially neither quite people nor animals. They sported the usual Mr. and Mrs. Potato Head bodies, hands, and feet, and also shared some accessories with the

Piggly Wiggly. Unlike "Juggle-Head," Mr. Potato Head would never wear animal parts, at least officially. Yet animal facial features began appearing in the Potato Head line in late 1953 or early '54, in their own, separate kits that made "Kitten Head, Bushy Bear, Dinkey Donkey, Piggly Wiggly, and many other favorite pets." The stage-like box contained thick, round foam heads and numerous spare accessories. Collection of Jeff Potocsnak. 10" by 14", "Spud-Ettes," Hassenfeld Bros., 1954.

Making Mischief. Only a year older than Mr. Potato Head, Hank Ketcham's "Dennis the Menace" panel cartoon was enjoying widespread popularity by the mid-1950s. This "Dennis the Menace Mischief Set" included a squirt flower, snake bow tie, fake spilled ink, fake bug, and fake cigarettes. Hassenfeld Bros. catalog, 1955 to later '50s.

heads of the family—not only eyes and eyebrows, but also hats, purses, and pipes.

Quite different, however, were the combined snout-and-mouth pieces, which took the place of the separate Potato Head nose-and-mouth pieces. The ears, too, were distinctly animal in nature. The resulting creatures, while close to the other Potato Heads in nature, bore charming animal names: Bushy Bear, Dinkey Donkey, Kitten Head, Puppy Pet, Honey Bunny, and Piggly Wiggly.

Hassenfeld Brothers also encouraged children to make their own new pieces: "You can create your own accessories, too, by using materials such as paper, cardboard, and wire pipe cleaners for additional fun."

Hassenfeld Brothers launched its new "Spud-Ettes, The Potato Head Pets" in a window box with a design distinct from the earlier ones. This time, the cardboard carry-case had a circus theme, with the Spud-Ette staring from behind the bars of the circus wagon.

By 1956 Hassenfeld Brothers partially rectified the situation of having animal heads sitting atop human bodies. It started issuing the Spud-Ettes with one-piece plastic bodies more obviously animal-like. Issued in the usual brightly colored hard plastic, the bodies came in either a sitting-up position, with forepaws stretched forward, or in a sitting position with forelegs keeping the body braced upright. Even with these new bodies available, however, the Spud-Ettes that sold in later rack assortments would still feature the human bodies.

The year they acquired new bodies, the Spud-Ettes also defected from the Potato Head clan.

Spuds and Spud-Ettes. *The "New Super Fun Pak" included bodies for the Potato Heads, but not for the pets. The Spud-Ette bodies were drawn-in. Collection of Jeff Potocsnak. 10½" by 15½", Hassenfeld Bros., 1956.*

51

"Mr. & Mrs. Funny Face." *Collection of Jeff Potocsnak. 8½" by 7", Western Germany, late 1950s.*

German Mr. Potato Head. *Collection of Jeff Potocsnak. 7" by 7", Western Germany, 1950s or '60s.*

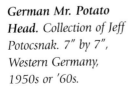

Cucumber Animal. *In the Potato Head universe, even the animals smoked pipes. In the 1954 box, three different Spud-Ettes were shown with pipes protruding. Hassenfeld Bros. catalog, 1955.*

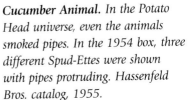

52

CAPTAIN KANGAROO'S PETS

In 1956, Hassenfeld Brothers decided to bank heavily on the popularity of a new children's TV sensation, the soft-spoken Captain Kangaroo, played by the former not-spoken-at-all Clarabelle of Doodyville on the Howdy Doody show. Bob Keeshan's CBS morning-show character was the opposite of a Clarabelle-type clown, being everyone's kindly uncle, not everyone's outrageously funny one.

To create a line of items bearing the Captain's name, Hassenfeld drew upon its extensive "Hasbro" play sets and activity kits. The new "Captain Kangaroo Shoe Box" was essentially a decorated and filled pencil box, with a full range of school and activity equipment. The Captain's "Kangadoodles," a plastic design kit, was based on Hasbro's popular activity set "Plasticubes," featuring colored plastic triangles that fit into a grid to form geometric patterns.

The previous "Hasbro Blackboard and Eras-O-Board Set" became "Captain Kangaroo's Eras-O-Board Set." The activity set called "Let's Play Conductor" became "Captain Kangaroo's Let's Play Conductor." Earlier "Play Clay" sets became "Captain Kangaroo's Play Clay."

Even the Potato Head clan was not immune from takeover. "Captain Kangaroo's Pets" featured three foam-headed "pets," otherwise known as Spud-Ettes. While the Spud-Ettes were obviously bigger news in their new guise, they still appeared in the three-dollar Potato Head set called the "New Super Giant Fun Pak." Despite this obvious connection to the Potato Head line, ads boasted that the Captain Kangaroo set "enables children to mimic Captain Kangaroo Pets, a daily feature of this outstanding show."

Naturally their new box displayed them in a cutout display that looked like the screen of a television.

Nothing could have been more indicative of Hasbro's faith in this new star than the fact that the Captain now appeared on pencil boxes. The Potato Heads disappeared.

The next year, the "Pets," along with the "Kangadoodles," disappeared from the Captain Kangaroo line—not because of any diminishing of the Captain's popularity, or of the Hasbro tie-ins to the show, which grew slightly in number.

The Captain's Plasticubes.
Popular in the earlier 1950s Hasbro line were "Plasticubes" plastic design craft kits. These kits involved a plastic frame in which triangular plastic tiles could be fit, resulting in colorful geometric patterns. When Captain Kangaroo was enjoying his first popularity in the mid-1950s, Hassenfeld Brothers adapted a number of its standard items to the times. "Plasticubes" became "Captain Kangaroo's Kangadoodles." Hassenfeld Bros. catalog, 1956.

Comical Combinations. *"'Potato Head' sets contain funny noses, eyes, ears, wigs, for comical combinations galore!" crowed Hassenfeld Bros. ads. "Use them on any fruit or vegetable! Each 98 cents." Woolworth's New Christmas Book, 1954.*

Carrot Critter.

The Captain's Pets. *While they had a new name on the outside of the box, inside the vegetable animals kept their old names: Kitten Head, Bushy Bear, Dinky Donkey, and Piggly Wiggly. Collection of Jeff Potocsnak; photo by Mark Rich. 10" x 14", "Captain Kangaroo's Pets," Hassenfeld Bros., 1956.*

Onion Oinker.

Hit at Any Party.
Booklets in "Mr. Potato Head" kits suggested not only different fruits and vegetables to use, but also the use of figures as party centerpieces and party favors. "Variations can also be made with clay," this booklet suggested, antici- pating the "Mister Funny Face" kits from Peerless Playthings. Collection of Jeff Potocsnak; photo by Mark Rich. Hassenfeld Bros., 1952.

Pepper Pooch.

■ ■ ■

"Selected as outstanding in their field by the Toy Guidance Council at the Toy Show last month … Two of our favorite people— Mr. and Mrs. Potato Head."
—*Hasbro Herald*, April, 1954.

■ ■ ■

SLIM DANDY SPECIALS

In 1956, Hassenfeld Brothers also introduced a new series of acetate-window display boxes, billing them as "Slim Dandy Specials."

Vertical boxes with three windows, they featured either the Mr. or Mrs. in the top window. A second foam head peered from the middle window. A display of extra accessories filled the bottom window. As before, the sets featured twenty-eight pieces each.

Mrs. Potato Head, in her third year, was being billed as a "fascinating individual! As sweet as a yam—tough as a turnip, or comical as a carrot … Complete feminine accessories, including a wig of real hair."

Also in 1956, the firm issued the "New Super Fun Pak," with the Mr. and Mrs. and two pets, and the "New Super Giant Fun Pak," with the complete family, including Spud, Yam, and two pets with their new, more animal-like bodies. These and the "Slim Dandy" sets would become the new standard packages.

Slim Dandy. New packages later in the 1950s continued offering the same number of parts as the original ones did, at the same dollar price. Collection of Jeff Potocsnak. 16½" tall, "Mr. Potato Head New Super Fun Kit," Hassenfeld Bros., 1956.

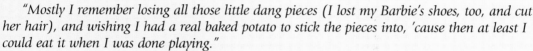

Later German Mr. Potato Head. Collection of Jeff Potocsnak. 7" by 7", Western Germany, 1950s or '60s.

IN THEIR POTATO HEAD DAYS

Imagine yourself in a lounge.
It is a virtual lounge.
The subject has turned to, of all things,
Mr. Potato Head.

"Mostly I remember losing all those little dang pieces (I lost my Barbie's shoes, too, and cut her hair), and wishing I had a real baked potato to stick the pieces into, 'cause then at least I could eat it when I was done playing."

—Nalo Hopkinson, resident of Toronto, Canada, and author of the richly imaginative novel *Midnight Robber* and short-story collection *Skin Folk*. She was five years old and living in Connecticut in her Potato Head days.

"I remember how old I am whenever I talk to a group of young'uns (defined as people under forty), tell them how I remember the days when Mr. Potato Head required an actual potato, and see the look of horror cross their faces. They're used to getting a plastic potato, but in the old days, all you'd ever get were the body parts, and then you'd have to beg your mom for a real potato, which would ooze all over your hands whenever you poked holes in it. Those were the days! Why in my day (grumble, grumble, grumble) ..."

—Scott Edelman of Damascus, Maryland, editor of the on-line *Science Fiction Weekly*, former editor of numerous magazines including *Science Fiction Age*, and author of several best-selling books on pro wrestlers. He lived in Brooklyn, New York, in his Potato Head days.

"I'm also from the 'needed a real potato' generation, and my mom would never give us one. We used Play-Doh instead. One time the three of us created a particularly spectacular monster from Play-Doh and Mr. Potato Head parts. Someone—I blamed my brother, and he blamed me; we'd have blamed our little sister, but there's no way Mom would have believed she could have operated the stove—decided to make it permanent by baking it. Those plastic pieces just don't hold up well in high temperatures ..."

—Amy Sheldon of Cleveland, Ohio, Internet junkie and benefits specialist. She was living in the Cleveland, Ohio suburb of Maple Heights in her Potato Head days.

"Plastic parts! When I was a kid there was no such thing as Mr. Potato Head. We had to make our own toys out of things we found on the floor of the cave."

—Richard Bowes of New York City, author of the prize-winning novel *Minions of the Moon*, and dedicated toy collector.

"Mr. Potato Head." Collection of Jeff Potocsnak. 10" by 7", English, late 1950s.

Leisure-time Mrs. Potato Head. In the 1950s, automakers tried hard to put women behind the wheel. They often suggested appropriate models by featuring them in magazine ads with a small side view of a gas pedal and a slender, high-heeled foot pushing it down.
By the end of the decade, Mrs. Potato Head got the message.
Mrs. Potato Head could now spend her leisure time in her hard-plastic car, hauling her shopping trailer. The car itself had a removable steering wheel. The wheels and axles were cast together as units. On the seat, two slotted pegs fit into the newly designed Potato Head body where the feet would normally go.
Mrs. Potato Head riding in her car with her original foam head. Hassenfeld Bros., 1959.
Photo by and collection of Mark Rich.

CHAPTER 5

ALTHOUGH NEITHER THEY
NOR ANYONE ELSE KNEW IT,
THE POTATO HEADS WERE ENTERING
THEIR LAST DAYS AS REAL POTATOES,
IN THE LATE 1950S AND EARLY '60S.

Or maybe they did—
For suddenly they were living in style: Cars, trailers, boats …
But weren't those balanced by their new domestic situation,
represented by the kitchen appliances and new vinyl baby?
Perhaps—But then what about Mr. Potato Head's locomotive engine?
Or his jet plane?

While a few years earlier Mrs. Potato Head sprang into being with two instant children, at the end of the 1950s she left those two firmly behind.

She did so by acquiring a new baby—a human one, at that, and of a clearly un-vegetable, vinyl nature.

The baby looked much like toy babies made to fit dollhouse toys. Its plastic sandbox and baby carriage were much like those found in tin dollhouses issued in great quantity and variety by Louis Marx.

Prior to this time, all Potato Head accessories were exactly that. They were accessories. They were to be put directly into a potato to create a toy, or else very closely attached to the potato, as in the case of Mrs. Potato Head's earrings, necklace, or purse. Everything else was left to the imagination and inventiveness of the playing child.

Now, however, auxiliary toys were appearing: household appliances, the baby, the baby's carriage, and a sandbox.

More importantly, powerful symbols of economic achievement and domestic ease appeared.

The Potato Heads now had cars.

A Riot of Fun. "Mrs. Potato Head with her new car and trailer is a riot of fun for every member of the family, regardless of age," the side of the box reads. "More amusing than ever!" The box could have boasted of itself, instead: "More beautiful than ever!" For collectors, these "driving" boxes rank at or near the top, in terms of their attractiveness. Collection of Jeff Potocsnak. 7½" by 10½", "Mrs. Potato Head," Hassenfeld Brothers, 1959–60.

58

Off Boating. *Mr. Jalapeño Head drives his car, with boat in tow. The Potato Head automobile was the first in the industry to be issued as an accessory to an existing toy character. Photo by and collection of Mark Rich.*

POTATOMOBILIA

In 1959, Mr. and Mrs. Potato Head succumbed to America's passion for the road.

Hassenfeld Brothers released new sets with autos: bright, hard plastic with rolling wheels. To get in and drive away, all Mr. and Mrs. Potato Head had to do was take off their feet and leave them at the curb. The "seats" of these potato-mobiles had pegs that fit into the leg-holes on the undersides of the Potato Head bodies.

The Potato Heads also needed new bodies, as it turned out. In Mr. Potato Head's original stance, his arms stretched wide, as if to show how big the world was. The same stance became Mrs. Potato Head's when she made her debut in 1952. Both stayed that way until it came time to leave feet on the sidewalk and drive away. With arms outstretched, how could Mr. Potato Head drive to fulfill his recreational needs, or Mrs. Potato Head, to fulfill her consumer destiny, except in the "Look Ma No Hands!" mode?

Hassenfeld Brothers

White Sky. *This less-common version of the Mrs. Potato Head box features a sky of plain, unpainted white. Canadian boxes appear to have been more commonly issued in these white-sky versions. Colored-sky versions may have been issued more in the East and South of the country, while white-sky versions appeared more often to the north and in Canada. Photo by and collection of Mark Rich. 7½" by 10½", "Mrs. Potato Head," Hassenfeld Bros., 1959–60.*

New Face of Hasbro. *After showing signs it would adopt Mr. Potato Head as the "face" of its toy line, Hassenfeld Bros. opted for the image of a young, smiling boy. Hassenfeld Bros. catalog, 1960.*

Hassenfeld Bros. catalog, 1962.

Responsible Mother. In this rare set, Mrs. Potato Head drives against a suburban background, as befit the suburban, new-family trappings she suddenly had: kitchen fixtures, sandbox, and baby carriage. A vinyl baby completed the picture. This large set measures 11" by 16". Collection of Jeff Potocsnak. "Mrs. Potato Head," Hassenfeld Brothers, 1959–60.

59

Potato Man of the World. At the end of the 1950s, Mr. Potato Head acquired all the trappings of success. Americans were spending heavily for leisure and entertainment. The popular potato man would not be left behind. Collection of Jeff Potocsnak. 7½" by 10½", "Mr. Potato Head," Hassenfeld Bros., 1959–60.

Mr. and Mrs. Potato Head are a happy family with their **NEW** baby—for more exciting play than ever before!

Everything Including the Kitchen Sink. New accessories arrived in the early 1960s. While Mrs. Potato Head looked pleased enough to be acquiring kitchen fixtures and a plastic baby, her husband must have felt beatific at abandoning his old-fashioned wheels for a trio of new transports: boat, train, and jet. Unlike the earlier boat trailer, the new boat was a vehicle of its own. Collection of Jeff Potocsnak. "Biggest All New Combination Pack," Hassenfeld Bros., early 1960s.

opted to change the Potato Head arms. The formerly short, outstretched stubs were now lengthened, even if the new length was to be held tightly against the body. Bent at the elbow, the hands now pointed forward.

Now the Potato Heads could drive.

Not very up-to-date in their choices, the Potato Heads got into flat-nosed convertible coupes, more reminiscent of the 1920s than the 1950s. Yet the hats, ties, hair ribbons, and overall orderly appearance the Potato Heads presented to the world had always suggested an old-fashioned and traditional approach to life. In adopting old flat-nosed Fords in glistening new plastic, they again were evoking a simpler time, when no one but a wealthy member of the Board of Trade could afford a car of any kind, and everyone else, kid and adult alike, could only turn and gawk.

In a real sense, however, the Potato Heads were not at all behind the times, and instead were very much on the cutting edge, introducing a new category of toy vehicle.

Toy cars were certainly nothing new, having been around as long as actual cars had been. By the 1950s, a number of companies existed with the primary purpose of producing toy cars. One such company was Chicago's Dowst Manufacturing

Hassenfeld Bros. catalog, 1960.

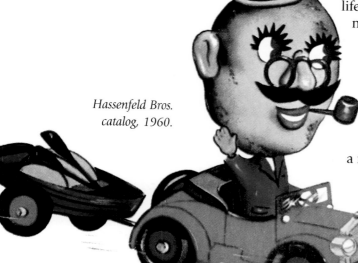

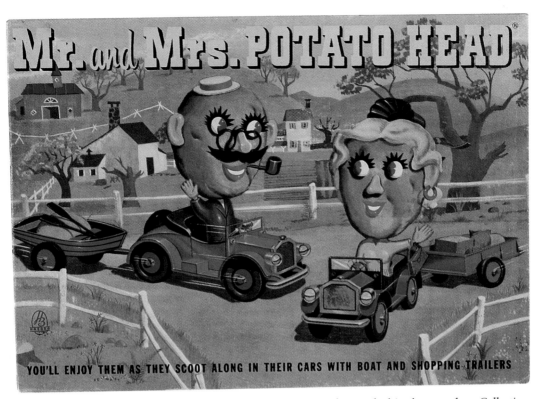

Family Travels. The Potato Heads never traveled in the same car, even when packed in the same box. Collection of Jeff Potocsnak. 14" by 10½", "Mr. and Mrs. Potato Head," Hassenfeld Bros., 1959–60.

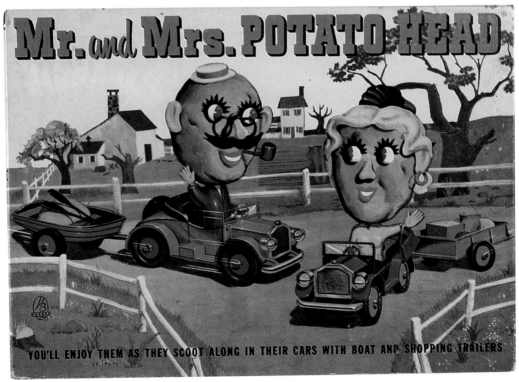

White Sky. While the blank background is the most obvious variation in this box, the box-top decorations also stop at the edge, instead of wrapping around to the sides. Collection of Jeff Potocsnak. 14" by 10½", "Mr. and Mrs. Potato Head," Hassenfeld Bros., 1959–60.

Nosh Noggin. The "Ice Pops" molds featured a ridge, seen below this buck-toothed character's chin, to hold the Popsicle stick in place. Collection of Jeff Potocsnak; photo by Mark Rich.

Frozen Confection Head. Collection of Jeff Potocsnak. 8" by 13½", "Mr. Potato Head Ice Pops," Hassenfeld Bros., late 1950s.

MR. FROZEN POTATO HEAD

In the late 1950s and early '60s, the Hasbro line expanded into food-making toys, including the "Hasbro Fizzies Fountain," for making and dispensing carbonated soda, and early "Frosty-Freez Ice Creamer" machines, for making ice cream and sherbet.

The "Frosty-Freeze," a plastic affair that looked a bit like a squat mailbox with a hand-crank on the side, would shortly transform into one of Hasbro's biggest hits of the early and middle 1960s, "Frosty Sno-Man Sno-Cone Machine." Being a toy that combined human features with a food item, Frosty Sno-Man had a more than passing kinship to Mr. Potato Head. The original "Frosty-Freez" continued to appear after Frosty Sno-Man's appearance in the early '60s, being repackaged in a Disney box as the "'Official' Mickey Mouse Club Ice Cream Machine."

The toy personality who preceded Frosty Sno-Man was, naturally, Mr. Potato Head. The "Mr. Potato Head Ice Pops" featured two molds for making frozen confections, one in red plastic and one in green. Both created funny-face ice-pops, looking nothing like Mr. Potato Head. No Potato Head images seem to have been used in connection with the sets, for whatever reason.

The flavoring for making the ice pops came in small envelopes, and could be eaten as candy. "Fun To Eat Lik-M-Aid Candy," the packages said. Besides orange, grape, and cherry, the ice pop packages came with plastic bags of "colored sprinkles" for jazzing up the frozen funny faces. Wood sticks and a plastic spoon, for the delicate act of mixing the flavored water, completed the kit.

And a Coupon, Too! The "Lik-M-Aid" packages in "Mr. Potato Head Ice Pops" were pushed for their versatility. "Try it!—on cereal, vegetables, apples, ice cream, cake icing, or cookies," the packages said. Once empty, each package became a coupon, to be sent in with "only 25 cents" for a "Lik-M-Aid Giant U.S. Wall Map," a "Lik-M-Aid Stamps" collection of 200 worldwide stamps, or a "Lik-M-Aid Paint Set." The "Lik-M-Aid" activity sets were likely not Hasbro sets, since the coupons were to be sent to Chicago. Collection of Jeff Potocsnak; photo by Mark Rich.

The First "Frosty." "Frosty Freez Ice Creamer," Hassenfeld Bros. catalog, 1960.

Company, owner of the already venerable "Tootsietoy" name. Another was London's Lesney Products, owner of the "Matchbox" name. Many other companies made toy cars a regular part of their product lines, including Louis Marx & Co., A. & E. Tool & Gage, Renwal Toy Corporation, Irwin Corporation, and the Hubley Manufacturing Company.

The Potato Head automobile, however, was a new idea in toy cars, for it was purely an accessory. True, some earlier play sets had appeared with toy cars, such as the service station play sets from Louis Marx and T. Cohn with plastic and metal toy cars, or the "RR" ranch sets by Louis Marx with plastic Nellybelles to go with realistic but tiny Roy Rogers figures. In these cases, however, the cars were not truly accessories, but an intrinsic part of the toy sets.

The new Mr. and Mrs. Potato Head auto was an accessory for a pre-existing, name-recognized set of toys. Nothing like it had appeared before. Probably the most similar toys were the various wheeled items produced to go with dolls, by various companies—not only doll buggies and carriages but even wheeled cribs, play tables, and shopping carts, such as those issued in the well-known "Doll-E-Toys" line of the 1950s.

They were not the same thing, however. While some dolls had acquired individual name recognition by the 1950s, such as the "Dy-Dee Baby" of Effanbee Doll Co. and "Betsy Wetsy" of Ideal Toy Corporation, they were typically baby dolls, and naturally were never given any accessories remotely like toy cars to ride in. Even with the growing interest in fashion dolls in the later 1950s, such as teen-age dolls "Jantzen" and "Sis-Teen" by Valentine Doll Inc., no toy or doll manufacturers had yet moved toward providing the figures with vehicle accessories.

The lack of such items reflects the lack of figural toys representing adults in the early postwar years.

When Mr. Potato Head appeared in 1952, he struck no jarring notes because he arose from the tradition of funny-face toys, not from the doll and figural toy tradition. Funny-face toys typically reflected adult features. While doll designers emphasized thin eyebrows, rounded cheeks, fat chins, and large eyes, designers of funny-face toys relied on the more extreme features to be found only in adult faces. Noses

In the Clouds. The "New Super Giant Fun Pak" was one of the last, if not the last, large-size, all-encompassing Potato Head sets to be issued. Collection of Jeff Potocsnak. Hassenfeld Bros., 1962.

63

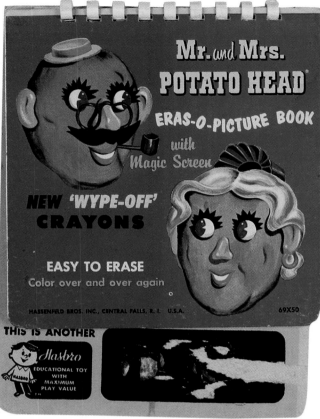

Eras-O-Picture. *The Hasbro toy line's rack assortments often included Potato Head items. The "Mr. and Mrs. Potato Head Eras-O-Picture Book," with "new Wipe-Off crayons," sold for 69 cents when it was introduced. Collection of Jeff Potocsnak. Hassenfeld Bros., 1960.*

When Good Spuds Go Bad. *Mr. Potato Head's makers undoubtedly fielded complaints about vegetables being turned into toys and then left in the toy box to rot. This remarkable pair of entombed tubers went the mummification route instead, with all their 1950s or early 1960s pieces intact. Collection of Jeff Potocsnak.*

were not funny unless big or misshapen. Funny hair, scraggly eyebrows, odd ears, warts, black eyes, and broken-toothed smiles—not to mention the wealth of hats, scarves, neckties, hairpieces, pipes, and eyeglasses—were all drawn from the world of the adult mug.

No one questioned that Mr. Potato Head was an adult. His name started, after all, with that "Mr.," and he rushed to get married and have children the year after his grand debut in fashionable society. His adolescent versions, Spud and Yam, were popular, but only because they were part of his entourage. They never had enough character to warrant packaging of their own, and were quickly eclipsed by the Potatoland pets, the Spud-Ettes.

Yet Mr. Potato Head was not just a funny-face toy. He was clearly a figural toy as well.

Mrs. Potato Head, with just enough accessories to make her look fashionable and smart, entered the scene when the country heavily favored a pretty-but-practical urban style. She, and not "Barbie," who appeared only when the Potato Head family was finally climbing into their hard-earned automobiles, was the first widely popular adult woman toy figure. She looked nothing like the fashion dolls of the later 1950s. Yet she stood closer to the original "Barbie" than did the fashion dolls "Jantzen" and "Sis-Teen," in one important sense. She was fully adult, and provided a miniature figure through which girls could play at being an adult woman—albeit a funny-faced adult woman.

Hassenfeld Brothers, in their approach to toy-making, had long emphasized the make-believe aspect of play. Make-believe, an essential part of childhood then as now, could be encouraged by providing the proper props. Doctor and nurse kits came first, as an outgrowth of a burgeoning business in producing school companions. Then, after the war, came other activity sets, including "Let's Play Conductor," "Let's Play Mailman," and "Let's Play School."

Mr. Potato Head appeared on the scene without any banners proclaiming its make-

Who Is that Mashed Man? *The Hasbro line contained a surprise one Halloween: a Mr. Potato Head costume, with both flexible plastic mask and a one-piece, jester-like suit. The similar Mrs. Potato Head costume featured a two-piece suit, with top and skirt. Collection of Jeff Potocsnak. Hassenfeld Bros., 1960.*

■■■

"Most criminal types can be helped by constructive hobbies such as woodcarving and Mr. Potato Head sets."

—Barney Fife, *The Andy Griffith Show*

■■■

Spud Spurs. *Children playing with "The Prairie Potato Head" kit had to ask their mothers for more than one potato. Making the horse required two all by itself. As did the "On Safari" Potato Head, this pipe-smoking cowboy packed a pistol. Collection of Jeff Potocsnak; photo by Mark Rich. "Prairie Potato Head," Peter Pan Series, England, mid-1960s.*

Change fruits and vegetables into funny lovable friends!

Change fruits and vegetables into funny lovable friends!

Age Ten. For the kit's 10th anniversary, the Potato Heads received colorful new boxes. While fanciful, they seemed a step backwards from the wonderful box designs from the beginning of the decade. Collection of Jeff Potocsnak. Hassenfeld Bros., 1962.

believe potential. Yet children had no figural toys depicting adults, except tiny play-set and doll-house figures, paper dolls, and immobile figures cast into tractors and other vehicles. None of these were of the scale of Mr. Potato Head, and many, such as the cast-in tractor drivers, exhibited no versatility.

Children absolutely loved playing at being adult. The success of Hassenfeld Brothers, Jack Pressman & Company, Transogram Company, Wornova Manufacturing Company, and other manufacturers with doctor and nurse kits, police and "G-Man" sets and outfits, sewing sets, and cowboy outfits certainly indicated this. Yet a parent could page through catalog after catalog, year after year through the 1950s, and find no freestanding figural toys clearly depicting adults, except Mr. and Mrs. Potato Head.

As the first figural toys of the generation to depict adults, they were also the first toy figures outside of dollhouses and miniature play sets to have accessories that suggested adult life. When the Potato Head automobiles arrived, they seemed utterly natural.

By 1959 Hassenfeld Brothers had years of manufacturing experience with toy cars. While many toy car collectors remain ignorant of the fact, the "Hasbro" name appeared on a small selection of vehicles: a white ambulance, dairy trucks that appeared in a variety of colors, red fire trucks, and two-tone police cars, all in hard plastic. While issued season after season, they had low visibility. They rarely appeared in packages of their own, and instead appeared as parts of games or activity kits. The games were all close in nature to play sets, having various small pieces and cardboard buildings to go with the vehicle toys: "Police Patrol," "Merry Milkman," and "Fearless Fireman" were among the names. The ambulances appeared in doctor and nurse kits and bags, vastly different in scale from the plastic medical equipment, but designed to encourage imaginative involvement with the idea of being a doctor or nurse. In the childhood play universe, scale is not always of paramount importance.

Scale never particularly mattered in the Potato Head universe, either. In fact, distortions of scale helped make the figures funny. A child using a big potato found the body's smallness all the more funny, or made the little hat on top all the more goofy.

In their own way, the cars fit. That they fit was all that mattered.

Cars were not all, however. So wealthy were the Potato Heads that Mr. Potato Head's car towed a boat trailer to demonstrate how much a man of leisure he now was. He had worked hard and long to earn profits for the Hassenfeld company, after all.

In turn, Mrs. Potato Head's car towed a small flatbed trailer. How else was she to cart home the results of all her shopping? She, too, had arrived, and was capable of acting as the perfect consumer.

Also symbolic of Mr. and Mrs. Potato Head's established status were the fading-away of Spud and Yam, who seemed to disappear with the last of the "New Super Fun Paks" in 1958–59.

The children had left the potato sack, and America's most famous vegetable couple turned to greet the new decade alone.

Sure, there was that plastic baby. But the baby looked nothing like a potato or any other changeable toy.

It simply did not count.

"Safari" kit interior.
Photo by Mark Rich.

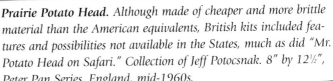

67

Prairie Potato Head. Although made of cheaper and more brittle material than the American equivalents, British kits included features and possibilities not available in the States, much as did "Mr. Potato Head on Safari." Collection of Jeff Potocsnak. 8" by 12½", Peter Pan Series, England, mid-1960s.

On Safari. "Mr. Potato Head" kits issued for children in England took off in some fascinating directions, such as in this big game hunting set. Mr. Potato Head sported the large, round, side-glancing eyes seen in earlier American sets, and had a body appropriately clothed in rugged wear. This included some features never seen in the States, including a hand clutching a pistol, a large safari hat, a machete, an axe, and a rifle. Collection of Jeff Potocsnak. "Mr. Potato Head on Safari," Peter Pan Series, England, mid to later 1960s.

Animal or Vegetable? The old question used in a game of charades
would have proved of no use to someone acting out "Mr. Potato Head."
The most popular game to actually feature the pipe-smoking vegetable,
however, was "Tooty Frooty." Released alongside plastic-head "Mr. Potato Head"
kits of the mid-1960s, it featured several new fruit and vegetable friends.
Collection of Jeff Potocsnak. Game spinner from "Tooty Frooty, the New
Mr. Potato Head Game," Hassenfeld Bros., 1964 to later 1960s.

CHAPTER 6

REMEMBER WHEN YOU COULD STOP ASKING MOM FOR VEGETABLES?

And when you could ask for a pepper by name?
Or a carrot? Or even a french fry?
It shows how accustomed we became to having a potato with a name,
that we took such food toys for granted when they
entered our lives as plastic toys.

P lastic faces had to arrive. With new thermo-plastics, the most versatile new materials for toy-making since the introduction of celluloid in the previous century, it was only a matter of time.

The old-fashioned materials, of course, worked fine for quite a while. "Changeable Charlie" relied on wood and lithographed paper, and did so for decades. The "Mr. Potato Head" kits needed only a potato, a situation that lasted a dozen years. "Wooly Willy" used a drawing on cardboard, and never budged from that most basic of approaches. Paper and board toys that came out of 19th-century traditions of sliced animals and changeable-face cards, such as the "Flip Faces" by Hassenfeld Brothers in 1963, also continued appearing.

Even a pegboard could work for a funny-face in a pinch, as Transogram proved when it issued "potato head parts" with its "Deluxe 9-in-1 Play Chest" in the late 1950s. Metal also served, as in 1958's "Eveready Magnetic Change-A-Face Wipe-Off Board." In this toy, a face similar to Mr. Potato Head's could be assembled on a metal blackboard. It did, of course, feature a pipe.

All-plastic funny-face toys were bound to appear, however, and were not slow in doing so. The plastic face-toy that may have been the first of the 1950s may also have been one of the most attractive: "Magnetic Comic Faces," which made its debut in early to mid-decade.

Mr. Plastic Head. *This colorful and appealing character with a plastic head may have been the first of the free-standing funny-face toys. The toy's combination of shiny plastic head, magnetic features, and both cardboard and flannel accessories, including a cardboard pipe, helped make it one of the most attractive toys of its kind. Collection of Jeff Potocsnak, photo by Mark Rich. "Magnetic Comic Faces," De Luxe Game Corporation, 1950s.*

Pure Magnetism. Even the box of "Magnetic Comic Faces" stood out with its excellent graphics and bright colors—for good reason. The artist's signature, "Eisner," appears just left of center, beneath the pipe-smoking gentleman. By the time "Magnetic Comic Faces" appeared, Will Eisner had left behind his famous comic character, the Spirit, to concentrate on his American Visuals Corp., creating cartoons and illustrations for both commercial and educational use. Collection of Jeff Potocsnak. De Luxe Game Corporation, 1950s.

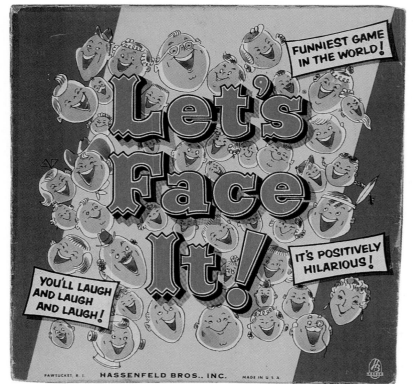

Face It. When the first Potato-Head-related game came out, it was close in nature to Schaper's popular "The Game of Cootie." Instead of dice, it employed a spinner for determining which parts of the game faces could be assembled. Collection of Jeff Potocsnak. 14½" by 14½", "Let's Face It!," Hassenfeld Bros., 1955–56.

MORE MAGNETISM

While "Juggle-Head" verged on the bizarre, another company took the same approach to produce a more appealing funny-face toy.

"Magnetic Comic Faces," by De Luxe Game Corporation of New York City, refined the "Juggle-Head" concept. Like the Langwood Products' toy, it had a fixed-shape head with embedded magnets for holding the facial features in place. It also employed some cardboard accessories.

The toy featured only the face, about six inches tall, with a flat back. Unlike Juggle-Head, the De Luxe head was made of pink, shiny, hard plastic. Nicely contoured, it had elevated cheekbones and forehead, and indented areas for the features.

Also unlike "Juggle-Head" it had an opening at the base, into which a wood dowel snugly fit. It came with both the dowel and a wood stand, the short dowel being painted dark blue, and the stand, red. The front of the stand had a slit cut into it. This served to hold the bottom edge of the cardboard body below the plastic face. The cardboard hats had strips stapled to their backs, for holding them atop the smooth head. While those strips would probably rip after a few uses, the overall design was otherwise sturdy and attractive.

The eyes were essentially the same as the "Juggle-Head" eyes. While superficially similar to Juggle-Head's features, the noses, ears, and mouths were engagingly distorted and malformed, adding to the comical effect. All of shiny plastic, the colors went beyond the usual range: not only red, yellow, and flesh-tones were represented here, but also pink, baby blue, and a milk-chocolate brown.

Surprisingly for a time when African-American style dolls were not unknown, and cross-racial understanding was being publicly encouraged, "Magnetic Comic Faces" seems to have stood alone in providing African-American options in its facial pieces.

Throughout the decade, similar toys continued to appear from miscellaneous manufacturers. Among them was "Magnetic Funny Faces," possibly made by De Luxe. The 1959 toy combined characteristics of both Juggle-Head and "Magnetic Comic Faces," having a molded face of "high impact plastic" and facial features that included animal snouts.

Krazy Ikes. Another 1955 game involved players taking turns assembling a creature, and likewise employed a spinner device. Photo by and collection of Mark Rich. Spinner from "Ike-A-Doo," Whitman Publishing Co., 1955.

LET'S FACE IT

Hassenfeld Brothers, tossing about for ways to capitalize on the success of "Mr. Potato Head" kits, issued its first all-plastic funny-face toys at the mid-point of the decade.

"Let's Face It!" was the first variation on the Potato Head theme. An activity game, "Let's Face It!" featured a board with a spinner at the center. The spinner arrow pointed to various facial features to be attached to one of four plastic faces. These faces sat atop cardboard bodies that could be propped up in each of the board's four corners. Looking appropriately potato-like, these faces had room for mouth, eye, nose, hat, and ear pieces, along with such flannel accessories as eyebrows and mustaches. The pieces, of course, were Mr. Potato Head pieces.

Since the game involved little more than taking turns at the spinner and trying to be first in

Big Face. In contrast to "Let's Face It!" the next funny-face game in the Hasbro line lasted only one season. Here, the plastic clown-face board is shown with all facial pieces in place. One of the aims of the game was to complete the face. Photo by and collection of Mark Rich. "Big Mouth," Hassenfeld Bros., 1957.

Allan Apple. Probably the most common approach to appropriating the Potato Head idea involved simply choosing a different fruit or vegetable for the name. In this case, an apple took the title. Collection of Jeff Potocsnak. "Allan Apple and His Garden Friends," unknown manufacturer, probably 1960s.

Sprung Spuds. The "Jumpin" Mr. and Mrs. Potato Head kits featured large, spring-run, wind-up bodies. Now blue-collar in his occupation, Mr. Potato Head chipped away with his steam drill, went fishing, or flew a kite, while the Mrs. cleaned and dusted, popped popcorn, and rang the dinner bell. Her kit gave the first indication the Potato Heads might eat other vegetables. Collection of Jeff Potocsnak. 15½" by 7", Hassenfeld Bros., 1966.

72

TV Stars Again. These large, nine-inch figures proved effective subjects in TV ads. "As Seen on TV" had the same influence on consumers the notice "As Advertised in Life" did a decade before. Collection of Jeff Potocsnak. Hassenfeld Bros., 1966.

constructing a funny face, it offered nothing that wasn't already available in "The Game of Cootie," made by W. H. Schaper Manufacturing Company of Minneapolis, Minnesota. In "Cootie," players tossed the die on the table. If one spot came up, you acquired a body. With two spots, you had a head. A certain amount of die-tossing frustration inevitably added to the interest of this simple assembly game. Whoever lucked first upon a die-toss with the single spot face-up had first pick of the Cootie body and was off to a head start. Assembly then became more difficult. The player had to roll the numbers three and four twice, to get the requisite pairs of eyes and antennae, and, most frustrating of all, the number six a total of six times. Number six naturally represented the number of Cootie's insect legs.

As with "Let's Face It!" the first person to assemble their Cootie bug was the winner. "The Game of Cootie," introduced in the late 1940s, had going for it the novelty of the insect being put together. By 1955, most kids knew what a plastic Cootie looked like, and enjoyed its high-style plastic oddness. It was a work of art that happened to be a toy.

Oddly enough, even with three years of success at selling Potato Head kits behind it, Hassenfeld Brothers opted out of calling their new game "The Mr. Potato Head Game," or otherwise identifying the game with the company's top-selling toy.

In the same year that the company introduced "Let's Face It!" another spinner-based game made its debut. In "Merry Milkman," the object of the game was to load small plastic representations of milk, butter, and eggs onto plastic dairy trucks, and to get them to their destinations. While "Let's Face It!" lasted only two seasons, "Merry Milkman" continued as a lead item in the Hasbro toy line into the next decade.

The company's next all-plastic funny-face toy likewise enjoyed only a short life. Introduced in 1957, "Big Mouth" combined the attractions of a funny-face toy with a word game. For the funny face, the board was a shaped-plastic surface, featuring the raised-plastic face of a clown, with indentations

Jumpin' Again. Collection of Jeff Potocsnak. 5" by 9", "Jumpin Mr. Potato Head," Hassenfeld Bros., 1967.

where various plastic facial features could be placed. Those facial features—mustache, eyes, ears, mouth, nose, bow tie, and hat—looked quite familiar.

The lower part of the board had four lines of square spaces, on which the words for the facial features appeared, and onto which letter tiles could be placed. In this, it was strongly reminiscent of Selchow & Righter Company's top-selling game, "Scrabble," introduced the same year as "The Mr. Potato Head Funny-Face Kit."

The funny-face toy with plastic face disappeared from the Hasbro toy line until 1964, when it returned with a vengeance. The large clown face as the focus of games and activities, however, would return a little earlier to the Hasbro line, in the "Corky Clown Big Top Circus Game" of the early '60s.

73

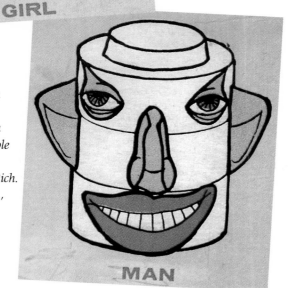

GIRL

MAN

Tower of Faces.
The "Doozies" foam
headpieces could be
stacked, making it a
changeable totem-pole
toy. Photos by and
collection of Mark Rich.
Kenner Products Co.,
1960s.

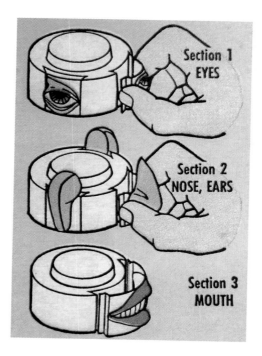

Section 1
EYES

Section 2
NOSE, EARS

Section 3
MOUTH

DOOZIES

Some of the oddest funny-face toys appeared in 1960 from Kenner Products Company of Cincinnati, Ohio.

Among the leading toy makers of the Baby Boom years, Kenner was issuing a popular line that had some emphasis on craft and art sets. The "Presto-Paints" and "Fountain Brush" paint sets were aimed at the same young-artist market as Hassenfeld Brothers' "Beaux Arts" and "Studio Art" kits. The company was having its greatest success with construction toys, however, ranging from the "Battery Motor" play drills to the highly popular "Girder & Panel" and "Bridge and Turnpike" sets.

Kenner entered the 1960s with a half-dozen new entries, mostly based on already successful products. "Sparkle Paints" and "Presto-Sparkle Paint and Coloring" sets expanded the art line. The battery-operated "Show Time Projector" made its debut, anticipating one of Kenner's great hits of the later '60s, the "Give-A-Show Projector." The firm's construction kits also went electric, with the "Motorized Girder Building and Bridge" sets. Its line of mobiles and other colorful attention-getters for infants grew with "Musical Nursery Birds" and "Firefly, the Light-Up Crib Exerciser."

Receiving less fanfare at its entrance was a put-together face toy sold in narrow cardboard boxes almost a foot and a half tall: "Doozies."

"Builds Thousands of Funny Faces 4-at-a-time. Easy To Do!" the box boasted, showing illustrations of the toy made into clown, pirate, girl, and man.

As was the case with the earlier Potato Head sets, "Doozies" had foam at their heart, or head. In this case, however, the foam was never meant to be replaced by a vegetable. The new kit used stacking, interlocking disks of foam. Usually three at a time went into a funny face, or all twelve, if you wanted to stack the faces together into a foot-high totem pole.

Twenty-four brittle plastic facial pieces—the usual mix of eyes, noses, ears, hair, and mouths—fit into slots cut into the sides of the cylindrical columns. The pieces could only fit in particular disks, however. Some disks, meant for the top of the head, had two slots, designed to hold the eyes. The central foam disk had a middle slot for the nose, and two side slots for the ears. The bottom disk had one large slot for the mouth.

These sets likely enjoyed a short time in the stores. No more than a toy for the momentary diversion of children, it had little chance of gaining any deep popularity. Its lack of flexibility, with facial features fitting only in predetermined places in the "heads," severely limited the creative options the kits gave kids. In this way, a "Doozies" set was more closely akin to the later Potato Head sets, which came with plastic vegetable heads and pre-punched holes for the facial features.

Kenner didn't help the toy's limited appeal by making it of such fragile materials. While foam has never ranked among the most durable of materials, it held up remarkably well compared to the facial pieces, made of easily cracked and broken vacuum-formed sheets of thin plastic.

Sophisticated Susie. "Help our spy friend out of this dangerous spot," says the back of the toy. "With your assistance even this top secret agent can assume a great many more and better disguises." Smethport steadily issued "Wooly Willy" kits through the decades, occasionally adding such timely items as "High Spy," a take-off on TV glamour-girl spies and the Bill Cosby vehicle, I, Spy. Collection of Jeff Potocsnak; photo by Mark Rich. 7" by 9", Smethport Specialty Co., 1966 and later years.

Changeable Popeye. Probably the star of the "Doozies" line was the "Popeye Doozies" set, featuring vacuum-formed pieces that assembled to create Popeye, Brutus, and Olive Oyl. Collection of Jeff Potocsnak. Kenner Products Co., 1960.

Chip off the Old Spud. Copycat Potato Heads appeared even from creditable firms, such as this kit from a New-York-City-based manufacturer known for its low-cost plastic bubble pipes, spring-powered "action toys," and novelties. Collection of Jeff Potocsnak. "Mr. and Mrs. Funny Face," Elmar Products Co., 1960s.

Mr. Egg-Bodd. Detail of box. Collection of Jeff Potocsnak; photo by Mark Rich. Box 6½" by 9", Peter Pan Playthings, 1960s.

Mr. Egg Head. Changing his alias from Mr. Egg-Bodd, Mr. Egg-Head could either sit in his red, soft-plastic egg cup or stand up in it, with legs fitting into the under-side of the cup. These sets, unlike the 1950s English sets, had their hands molded into the soft-plastic bodies. Only the feet needed to be attached. Collection of Jeff Potocsnak; photo by Mark Rich. Box detail. 9" by 10", Peter Pan Playthings, 1960s.

Mr. Egg-Bodd and British Mr. Potato Head. Never introduced in the United States, Mr. Potato Head's friend Mr. Egg-Bodd enjoyed life as an English toy. Collection of Jeff Potocsnak; photo by Mark Rich. Peter Pan Playthings, England, 1960s.

British Lady. While this box featured real fruits and vegetables on the top, the kit did come with a plastic head. Collection of Jeff Potocsnak. "Mrs. Potato Head," Merit, England, 1960s or '70s.

British Spud. *Collection of Jeff Potocsnak. "Mr. Potato Head," Peter Pan, England, 1968.*

Mr. Hong Kong Face. *Many low-end companies survived by issuing mysterious copies of popular toys, with the minimal required markings—in this case, simply "Hong Kong." Collection of Jeff Potocsnak. Unknown manufacturer, probably 1960s.*

POTATO HEADS TRAVEL THE WORLD

Thanks to a combination of licensing deals in some countries and outright toy-idea piracy in others, Potato Head toys flourished overseas. Even his licensed versions, however, sometimes seemed quite different from the American originals.

El Señor. *Versions of "Mr. Potato Head" appeared in many other countries. Collection of Jeff Potocsnak. 4" by 2", "El Sr. Patata," Mexico.*

Mexican Uncle. *"Tus nuevos amigos de la Familia Ledy Gumbres." The "Tio Papa" kits of Mexico had photographic boxes, unlike the equivalent versions in the States. Collection of Jeff Potocsnak. Mexico, 1960s.*

MR. POTATO HEAD'S PLASTIC MAKE-OVER

Some of the biggest toys of the decade would make their first appearances in 1964, fighting their way to shares of the market with constant barrages of bright, happy, and noisy Saturday-morning TV commercials.

At least three new toy names would become famous. Kenner introduced its "Easy-Bake Oven." Louis Marx introduced the "Rock'Em Sock'Em Robots." Tonka Toys introduced its "Mighty Tonka Dump Truck." Other manufacturers vied for attention, including Mattel with its "V-rroom!" line and De Luxe Reading Corporation with its "Johnny Seven One Man Army" gun.

A few companies were glowing with success, having a year of unprecedented profits behind them. This was the case with Ideal Toy Corporation, which had led the toy world with its hit "Mouse Trap" game.

A few others were licking their wounds, as was the case with Hassenfeld Brothers, which had released the seemingly sure-fire success "Flubber" in 1963. A substance somewhat like the popular "Silly Putty," it was a tie-in item, linked to the popular Walt Disney movies of 1961 and '62, *The Absent-Minded Professor* and *Son of Flubber.*

Tooty Frooty Farewell. *These photo-art boxes appeared with the last of the "Tooty Frooty Friends." Collection of Jeff Potocsnak. Hassenfeld Bros., 1972.*

Katie & Pete. *Mr. Potato Head's plastic friends enjoyed playground fun on these, the most attractive of the Tooty Frooty Friends boxes. Collection of Jeff Potocsnak. Hassenfeld Bros., 1966.*

"Flubber" turned out to be less "trouble-free to parents" than expected. More unfortunately, it also turned out to be less "non-toxic to kids" than the company thought.

Hassenfeld Brothers, while suffering from low profits and mounting lawsuits, managed to pull out of its difficulties. Moreover it joined Kenner, Marx, and Tonka in introducing a toy name in 1964 that would become famous: "G. I. Joe." While putting considerable energies into developing and then keeping up with demand for this popular doll, the company was also revamping the "Mr. Potato Head" kits.

Now, instead of a box that seemed almost empty because it only had little plastic pieces for sticking in real potatoes, children could open a box and find those pieces and the potato, made out of safe, hygienic polyethylene. The new toy potatoes were hollow shells of brown plastic, with holes in appropriate places for hat, eyes, nose, mouth, pipe, and ears, and for the neck of the body.

While it probably pleased those parents dismayed by wasted food, the appearance of plastic heads in the "Mr. Potato Head" line of activity kits signaled the beginning of the end for one of the most creative, and creativity-inspiring, toys of the Baby Boom years.

Mr. Potato Head, instead of being a charac-

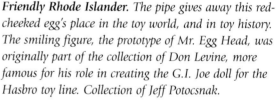

79

Friendly Rhode Islander. *The pipe gives away this red-cheeked egg's place in the toy world, and in toy history. The smiling figure, the prototype of Mr. Egg Head, was originally part of the collection of Don Levine, more famous for his role in creating the G.I. Joe doll for the Hasbro toy line. Collection of Jeff Potocsnak.*

Cooky & Oscar. *Collection of Jeff Potocsnak. Hassenfeld Bros., 1966.*

Tooty Frooty Friends. The first versions of the Tooty Frooty Friends boxes featured simpler artwork and white backgrounds. They also appeared in boxes with cellophane windows at the bottom. Collection of Jeff Potocsnak. Hassenfeld Bros., 1964.

For Total Fruit Cases. The new plastic heads for the Potato Head clan worked wonderfully in game format. Its charm and simplicity won over more children's hearts than did the earlier "Let's Face It!" Collection of Jeff Potocsnak. "Tooty Frooty Game," Hassenfeld Bros., 1964 and later '60s.

ter created by each child, was now only a toy. From a toy of infinite possibilities, available only the year before, it had been reduced to a toy of only a few.

Introducing the plastic-heads to the kits did help take the toy out of the kitchen. It also allowed Hassenfeld Brothers to establish some new, specific characters.

With the older sets, children would take the same accessories and attach them to any vegetable or fruit from the fridge. Any vegetable became, in essence, "Mr. Potato Head," because Mr. Potato Head was a character made of the accessories that were inserted into the vegetable or fruit, and not the vegetable or fruit itself.

With the new plastic "heads," this all changed. Names could be assigned to specific items. Mr. Potato Head now had his "Tooty Frooty Friends," whose names were Pete the Pepper, Oscar the Orange, Cooky the Cucumber, and Katie the Carrot. In this new series, Mrs. Potato Head disappeared, for the time being. The new, no-hair Cooky and Katie took her place.

These individual characters each came with a Mr. Potato Head toy, in his new plastic-head incarnation. The paired sets remained in the reasonable one-dollar bracket, while the combination kit, "Mr. Potato Head and his Tooty Frooty Friends," cost two dollars.

Costing yet a dollar more was "Tooty Frooty, the New Mr. Potato Head Game." The new game box contained a spinner dial and four compartments for pieces, with enough accessories for building Mr. Potato Head and three of his new friends.

The spinner showed a buck-toothed Potato Head at its center, jaunty in his red cap.

Although no more complicated than "Let's Face It!" the new game had more visual charm than did the old. Each of the separate vegetable beings could be held by the playing children. It was a game, and also a box of toys.

Meet the New Friends. *As irresistibly charming as it is rare, this store display announced the rise of non-vegetable foods to the Potato Head pantheon. Collection of Jeff Potocsnak. 26" by 16", Hassenfeld Bros., 1966.*

Picnic Pals. *On this rare box, Willy Burger seems to take Frankie Frank's side against Frenchy Fry. Collection of Jeff Potocsnak. 9" by 6" by 4", "Mr. Potato Head Presents His Picnic Pals," Hassenfeld Bros., 1966.*

New ... Different ... Exciting! *While the move to plastic heads did reduce the possibilities inherent in the Potato Head line, Hassenfeld Bros. made up for it by introducing a set of attractive new characters. This selection appeared in two different boxes. Collection of Jeff Potocsnak. "Mr. Potato Head's Tooty Frooty Friends," Hassenfeld Bros., 1964.*

A Crooked Guy. *Frenchy Fry, 8″ tall, appears with Mr. Soda Pop Head, 6″ tall, and Mr. Potato Head. Mr. Soda Pop Head had the longest name in Potato Head land. Collection of Jeff Potocsnak. Hassenfeld Bros., 1966.*

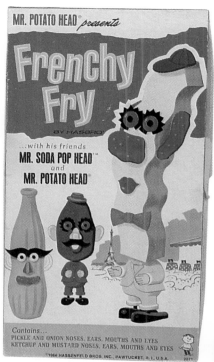

Suave Sausage. *Frankie Frank, 9″ tall, appears with his friends Mr. Mustard Head, 3½″ tall, and Mr. Potato Head. Collection of Jeff Potocsnak. Hassenfeld Bros., 1966.*

THESE FRIENDS FEATURED
THE LINE'S FUNNIEST FACES ...

... AND REFLECTED AMERICA'S
INCREDIBLE LOVE OF FAST FOOD.

FINALLY A FRENCH FRY

During the Baby Boom years, people still lived in what we might call the french-fry frontier of diner dining: the menus of McDonald's and Burger King had not become de rigueur cuisine for America's youth; and trademarked greasy, salty, sugar-coated, slender fries were not yet an emblem of a nation's sacrifice of facial complexion to the god of corporate profits.

When we look back on the 1966 Hassenfeld Brothers innovations of "Willy Burger" and "Frankie Frank," we immediately think they must have been food premiums, issued with various kid's meals. Yet when Hassenfeld Brothers introduced these toys, they were nothing less than that: toys. They had no promotional tie-in. They had no fast-food connection. They suggested no endorsements and no compromises.

Hamburgers, franks, french fries, catsup, and mustard still appeared in everyday home-cooked meals in 1960s American households. While few mothers made their own sausages and wieners anymore, countless millions made and flipped burgers.

When Hassenfeld Brothers introduced its "Picnic Pals," each kit offered a "main character." Who might take starring roles in the world of the American diner and home-grilled cuisine? Figures of burgers, hot dogs, and french fries, of course. These became the new food-based personalities of Willy Burger, Frankie Frank, and Frenchy Fry.

The new heads were made of soft plastic, in the tradition of the 1964 sets, and amusingly captured their various food models. New facial features also

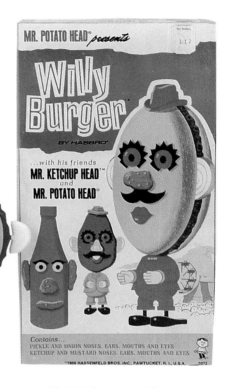

Old Pickle-Nose. Willy Burger, 7" tall, appears with Mr. Ketchup Head, 6" tall, and Mr. Potato Head. The characters based on condiments and a soda bottle were the first toys in the line to be based on packaging, not on the food itself. Collection of Jeff Potocsnak. Hassenfeld Bros., 1966.

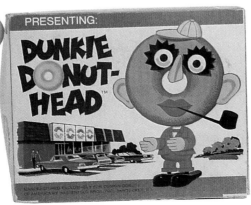

The New Mr. Spudnut. One of the most unusual of 1960s Potato Head toys was this fellow with a hole through his head, offered through Dunkin Donuts. The doughnut was a solid ring of foam. Collection of Jeff Potocsnak. 5" by 4" by 2½", "Dunkie Donut-Head," Hassenfeld Bros., 1960s.

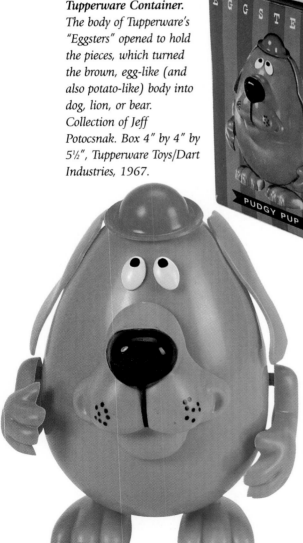

Not Just Another Tupperware Container. The body of Tupperware's "Eggsters" opened to hold the pieces, which turned the brown, egg-like (and also potato-like) body into dog, lion, or bear. Collection of Jeff Potocsnak. Box 4" by 4" by 5½", Tupperware Toys/Dart Industries, 1967.

■■■
LITTLE KNOWN TODAY, THE EGGSTERS WERE AHEAD OF THEIR TIMES.
■■■

played off of the culinary treats found in diners. Ears or noses might be pickles; ears and mouths might be onion slices.

Alongside these pickles and onion slices, old Mr. Potato Head pieces helped ground the new toys in familiarity. The hard plastic hats, beady eyes, flannel eyebrows and mustaches, and especially the bright, monochromatic plastic bodies, all looked the same. They also looked fitting. The baseball cap seemed especially appropriate atop the elongated noggin of that ballpark being, Frankie Frank while the neat bow tie looked exactly right on Frenchy Fry, the lone potato-based star of this new series.

Each main character came packaged with a "companion." As one might expect, these were based on catsup, mustard, and soda pop. Yet in their appearance, Mr. Ketchup Head, Mr. Mustard Head, and Mr. Soda Pop Head represented something new and different. For the first time in the Potato Head universe, characters were being based on food containers, rather than on the foods themselves. Even more strikingly, they were heads only, without the body that helped make Mr. Potato Head so charming.

They held a secondary but essential role, just as the catsup, mustard, and soda did in the real diner.

It may have been symbolic, or simply necessary for the unity of the Potato Head line, that the sets also included a third character: a Mr. Potato Head, smiling ambassador of everyday American existence.

Another of the most unusual characters in the Potato Head line appeared in the 1960s. Like Willy Burger and friends, it was a prepared-food personality. This time, however, it not only looked like a food premium, it clearly was one. "Dunkie Donut-Head" had all the usual Mr. Potato Head parts, from shoes, body,

and hands to eyes, nose, mouth, ears, cap, and, of course, pipe. Yet the head was a doughnut-tinted circle of foam, three and a half inches in diameter. The odd figure stood seven inches tall.

While issued by Hassenfeld Brothers, it never appeared in the Hasbro line. It could only be found at Dunkin Donuts of America outlets.

THE LOOK OF THE FUTURE

A toy from outside the Hassenfeld Brothers stable would prove prophetic of the direction Mr. Potato Head himself would be taking, some five years down the road.

In 1967, a year after the "Picnic Pals" appeared, people attending Tupperware parties had the chance to buy an entertaining funny-face toy.

The side of the box had the stylized motif of the circus wagon, as did the "Spud-Ettes" of the 1950s. Like the Spud-Ettes, too, these toys made animal figures: Pudgy Pup, Lumpy Lion, and Bulgy Bear.

While the Tupperware Toys "Eggsters" looked almost nothing like those 1950s Potato Head animals, they had several features that anticipated the Potato Heads of the 1970s. The head and body were joined in what the toy's name suggested was an egg, for all that it looked like a potato—especially the potato of 1970s and '80s Mr. Potato Heads.

The face pieces were a good bit larger than the traditional Potato Head pieces. They had blunt tips on the back, not sharp as in the Potato Head pieces of the 1950s and '60s. When not being played with, these pieces could be stored inside the body, which opened to hold them.

With the head and body being one egg-shaped piece, the feet connected directly to the bottom.

Circa 1970. Two plastic Potato Head figures. All of the features shown here are early ones. The classic, round eyes and Mrs. Potato Head's cardboard-brimmed hat were never issued with the all-plastic kits. Collection of Jeff Potocsnak.

Potato Roll. Toddlers could push themselves around on this wheeled potato, 18" long. It retained its funny-face aspect, with removable eyes, brows, nose, mouth, eyeglasses, hat, and ears. Unused pieces were stored beneath the saddle. Collection of Jeff Potocsnak. Mr. Potato Head riding toy, Hasbro Industries, 1973.

Famous Funny-Faces. While Mr. Potato Head's name appeared largest on these packages, anyone picking up these kits knew the guest stars were bigger draws. These kits did offer a good amount of fun, since the Bozo or Donald pieces could be interchanged with Mr. Potato Head's. Collection of Jeff Potocsnak. Boxes 11½" by 9", "Mr. Potato Head Plus His Friend Donald Duck" and "Bozo," Hasbro Industries, early 1970s.

Within a few years, Mr. Potato Head would have these features: the merged, egg-shaped head and body; larger pieces, all with blunt tips on the back; bodies that could hold the accessory pieces; and feet connecting directly to the combined head and body.

Called the "Three-in-One" toy, "Eggsters" could make a few, well-defined characters, each of whom were illustrated on the box.

The Potato Head line had taken a move in the direction of firmly defining its funny-face characters with the "Tooty Frooty" line. It would be taking further such moves in years to come.

LAST YEARS

By the mid-1960s, Hassenfeld Brothers catalogs no longer billed Mr. Potato Head as the nation's "Number One Toy." Maybe the fact that the company had deprived children of the excitement of playing with real food caused its decline. Through the years, Mr. Potato Head had settled through the toy ranks, going from being one of the brightest stars to being just one minor star of many. Even in the company's own catalogs he no longer took first billing.

Yet he remained an important part of the Hasbro line. As the 1970s rolled in, the same four basic kits continued appearing: Mr. Potato Head with Pete, Oscar, Cooky, and Katie. No new foodstuffs appeared.

Even so, some new faces did appear.

They looked radically different, even though they were designed to be popped atop Potato Head bodies. One toy made a Donald Duck figure. The other made a Bozo. As with the Tooty Frooty Friends, the famous pair came packed with a companion Potato Head. If such characters had entered the Potato Head pantheon in the 1950s or early '60s, they would have been real-potato toys, with Donald-looking or Bozo-looking features to be stuck into the head. These new figures were purely and simply Donald and Bozo, related to the Potato Head line mainly in their packaging.

Mr. Potato Head's declining status was visible elsewhere in the Hasbro line. Where in the late 1950s and early '60s it seemed natural that a Potato Head "Eras-O-Board" should appear, the early 1970s pencil-by-number sets only had more famous characters—not only Donald and Bozo, but also Superman, Lassie, Casper, Mary Poppins, Mickey Mouse, Winnie-the-Pooh, Popeye, and the Flintstones. Old tuber-head no longer qualified.

By 1972, the Tooty Frooty Friends seem to have largely vanished from the line, although a few kept appearing in larger three-figure packs with Donald and Bozo. To compensate, however, Mrs. Potato Head made her reappearance. Hasbro issued solo packages of the Mr. and Mrs. in separate boxes, using identical plastic potatoes for heads and essentially the same variety of plastic pieces used since the 1950s.

In addition, three odd new figures briefly appeared: "Mr. Potato Fish," "Mr. Potato Bird," and "Mr. Potato Bug." Called the "Potato Pals," these sets included some twenty-plus pieces each, and assembled into a fish that needed to be held up on a plastic stand, a bird, and an insect.

Even if it was no longer the star line it used to be, the Potato Head idea still maintained some momentum and energy. It had seen several golden periods of creativity, first in the debut years of 1952 and '53, and then again in the mid-years of 1959 and '60.

A third period, as it happened, occurred in 1968, when a series of elaborate play sets involving real potatoes appeared, right in the middle of those first years of plastic-head toys.

Bird, Bug, and Fish. After the long absence of the Spud-Ettes, the Potato Head world briefly brimmed with new animal life in the early 1970s. Collection of Jeff Potocsnak. 9" by 5" boxes, "Potato Pals" series: "Mr. Potato Bug," "Mr. Potato Bird," and "Mr. Potato Fish," Hasbro Industries, 1972.

87

Funny but Dangerous. *The light-hearted and typically 1970s designs on these boxes give no indication of the storm of controversy surrounding the toys inside. Toys of many kinds were being attacked because of the risks they presented to children. Mr. Potato Head was singled out for its small, sharp-tipped parts. These boxes for Mr. and Mrs. Potato Head heralded the end of an era. The next year, an almost entirely different toy would be unveiled. Collection of Jeff Potocsnak. Hasbro Industries, 1972.*

Mr. Peel Armstrong. *A year before Neil Armstrong's boot left its first print on the Moon, a tail-finned cucumber landed there with a tuberous crew. Here the intrepid explorer is startled by an encounter with an alien shallot. The surface of the Moon turns out to be not green cheese, but instead covered with vegetables. Collection of Jeff Potocsnak; photo by Mark Rich. Hasbro Industries, 1966.*

CHAPTER 7

ON THE MOON ...
IN THE PARADE ...
AT THE CIRCUS ...
IN FANCY GET-UPS AT THE MASQUERADE ...

AFTER YEARS OF HARD WORK, AND
THEN A COUPLE YEARS OF VACATION,
REAL POTATOES CAME BACK IN 1968,
AND HAD SOME SERIOUS FUN.

After the decisive step toward all-plastic kits at mid-decade, Hassenfeld Brothers, now calling itself Hasbro Industries, made a return in 1968 to its literal roots: toys that required real vegetables and fruit for their proper enjoyment.

"Ask Mom to give you any fruit or vegetable," Hasbro again instructed its young customers. The instructional materials must have been exciting for kids, since kids the year before had found plastic potatoes beneath the Christmas tree. Fresh onions, cucumbers, potatoes, peppers, and apples were all fair game again.

The new play sets were designed to create at least three characters at a time, with one of the "characters" often being a vegetable vehicle or a large animal.

These new sets had a tendency to prescribe which fruits or vegetables to use for each particular character—much more so than in the 1950s and early '60s.

The remarkable "Mr. Potato Head on the Moon" kit called for a cucumber to turn into a space ship, a potato to be the astronaut, and an onion for the "space character." The first extraterrestrial funny-face to appear in the Potato Head series, the Potato Head alien, may also have been the first such character to appear after the "Space Faces" alien of the early 1950s.

"Mr. Potato Head on the Railroad" again called for a cucumber for the vehicle. This time it served as a locomotive, with a potato becoming the engineer, and an orange, the "workman,"

On the Moon. *Mr. Potato Head embarked on his greatest adventure in his only Space Age kit. Collection of Jeff Potocsnak. "Mr. Potato Head on the Moon," Hasbro Industries, 1968.*

in coal-shoveling garb.

"Mr. Potato Head in the Parade" once more called for a cucumber, this time for a different kind of wheeled object: the calliope. A lemon was to serve for the majorette, and an onion for the clown.

The "Mr. Potato Head on the Farm" kit called for a carrot to provide the Potato Head transportation. The carrot became a horse. A potato

Space Spud and Alien Shallot.
Photos by Mark Rich.

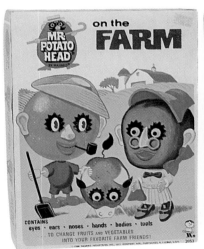

90

became the cow; an orange, the farmer; and a pepper, "Mrs. Old MacDonald."

At the same time, Hasbro issued larger play sets. These contained eighty pieces against the thirty-five of the three-character kits. Part of the charm of these large sets came from cardboard backdrops that unfolded into colorful scenes appropriate to each kit.

Against a desert backdrop featuring frontier-city store-fronts, the "Mr. Potato Head Wild West Play Set" called for potatoes to transform into a stagecoach and a cow. A green pepper became the bandit, while an onion served for the Indian.

Perhaps the most adventurous set after "Mr. Potato Head on the Moon" was the "Mr. Potato Head Masquerade Play Set," with its backdrop of a decorated ballroom. The kit called for such grocery staples as a pear to take on pirate disguise, an onion to be the witch, and a potato to be the clown.

The funniest of the play sets, however, may have been the "Mr. Potato Head Circus Play Set." Calling for a cantaloupe and orange for the rotund elephant, it also required a cucumber for the weight-lifter, two lemons for the weight-lifter's barbells, and onions or oranges for the clowns, all of whom cavorted before the backdrop of the Big Top tent.

Hassenfeld Brothers issued another play set, in the same year, that hearkened back to the past in a different way. Rather than calling for actual fruits and vegetables, it relied entirely on foam heads. Called the "Funny Mooners," it used pieces from the "Mr. Potato Head Circus" and other play sets. Added to the green foam pieces, they created monsters.

The return to potato-based kits was short-lived. Hasbro turned back to all-plastic kits as it closed the 1960s and entered the 1970s, the decade when Mr. Potato Head would go through a total transformation. Soon he would leave his 1950s character behind him for good.

On the Job. *Until the 1960s, Mr. Potato Head seemed a fairly ordinary soul, the sort of vegetable personality you might greet with a friendly wave without ever knowing his precise occupation. In the 1960s, he became a transient character, flitting from career to career. Besides visiting the Moon, Mr. Potato Head took part in parades, worked on the farm, and ran the railroads. These sets also introduced additional accessories, such as plastic tools for the farm kit or batons for the parade kit. Collection of Jeff Potocsnak. Boxes 9½" by 7", Hasbro Industries, 1968.*

Elephantaloupe. A cantaloupe makes the elephant; a cucumber, the muscle man; and a potato, the ringmaster-clown. A cardboard backdrop completes this scene built from a Potato Head play set. Collection of Jeff Potocsnak. Hasbro Industries, 1968.

NUMBER ONE FELT TOY

The following instructions could be found in kits of the late 1960s, when Hasbro Industries feared that the complications of assembling a full circus or masquerade set might prove confusing.

Please follow the assembly instructions [that] pertain only to the felt accessories that are enclosed in your set.

- The cow tail, horse tail, Indian head band, stage coach door, and eye patch are held in place with a common pin.

- The red neckerchief, cape, skirt and witch's dress are held in place by the point on the body. Put a rubber band around the witches dress to hold it in place.

- The red mask & pirate's beard are held in place by the ears.

- The black beard is held in place by the mouth.

- The mask is held in place by the eyes.

- The trim for the float is held in place by the round eyes.

- The daisy is assembled with the long plastic pin.

- One end of the tether cord is held in place by looping it and slipping it over the top prong in back of the space helmet. The other end is held in place with a common pin.

"Circus Play Set" and *"Masquerade Play Set."*
Collection of Jeff Potocsnak. Hasbro Industries, 1968.

92

Romper Room Mr. Potato Head by **Hasbro.**

Featuring Mr. Potato Head's
Happy Holiday Friends
Santa Claus • Halloween Goblin • Easter Rabbit

...with full color Romper Room Holiday scene!

Happy Holiday Friends. This unusual and hard-to-find play set featured a trio of holiday figures rarely brought together in any single set of any kind, since they represent widely separated parts of the year. Like the 1968 kits, this one called for real fruit and vegetables. Collection of Jeff Potocsnak. Hasbro Industries, early 1969.

SILLY BILLY

The decade that saw Hassenfeld Brothers increasingly backing away from the use of real potatoes saw other companies moving into the real-potato niche.

While a great many such kits probably appeared in surprise packages, midway and carnival prize assortments, and bargain-store rack selections, some did appear in attractive boxed sets. One such was "Silly Billy, the Fruit and Vegetable Man."

The Tot Guidance division of Multi-State Industries of Newark, New Jersey, a minor but established player in the educational toy field, was its manufacturer. The company specialized in magnetic blackboards, pull toys, plastic beads, and toy clocks.

In releasing "Silly Billy," it made little if any attempt to disguise its "Mr. Potato Head" type kit. The cover of the box showed a pair of children happily assembling Potato Head figures, using real potatoes, orange, onion, apple, and cucumber. A cardboard insert within the box also showed line drawings of different characters to be made, with a name under each one: Orange Head, Tomato Head, Pickle Head, Carrot Head, Onion Head, and, of course, Potato Head.

The "Silly Billy" pieces themselves were close enough to Mr. Potato Head's to seem direct copies. The contours of the eyeglasses and the shape and length of the pipe, for instance, seemed almost identical. Other items were only mildly different. Rather than being made of felt, the eyebrows and mustaches were made of a flannel-like thick paper.

The item in the kit most different from Mr. Potato Head was also the least significant: the head piece came as a foam sphere, not a rounded piece cut from a foam sheet.

MR. POTATO HEAD BY HASBRO

WILD WEST PLAY SET
Featuring Full Color Western Scene

CONTAINS Full Color Western Background Scene • Bodies • And Other Exciting Parts • To Make Your Potato Head *... At Home On The Range!*

"Wild West Play Set." Collection of Jeff Potocsnak. Hasbro Industries, 1968.

At the Parade. Collection of Becky Stubbe; photo by Mark Rich.

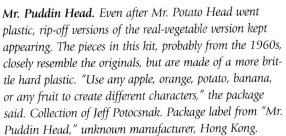

Mr. Puddin Head. *Even after Mr. Potato Head went plastic, rip-off versions of the real-vegetable version kept appearing. The pieces in this kit, probably from the 1960s, closely resemble the originals, but are made of a more brittle hard plastic. "Use any apple, orange, potato, banana, or any fruit to create different characters," the package said. Collection of Jeff Potocsnak. Package label from "Mr. Puddin Head," unknown manufacturer, Hong Kong.*

Still Funny. *Rip-off Potato Head kits such as these could appear as carnival prizes or in surprise packages, and thus evade notice. These appear to have been made by the same manufacturer as "Mr. Puddin Head." Collection of Jeff Potocsnak. "Funny Face Kits," Hong Kong, 1960s.*

Tomato Head and Onion Head. *Box detail, "Silly Billy," Tot Guidance, 1960s.*

The Fruit and Vegetable Man. *While the Hasbro line was emphasizing plastic heads for most of the decade, a few other companies moved into the real-vegetable arena. This close-up from the "Silly Billy" box, depicting a boy at play, shows how close this toy was to the old Mr. Potato Head. Collection of Jeff Potocsnak; photo by Mark Rich. 5½" by 8½", "Silly Billy," Tot Guidance, 1960s.*

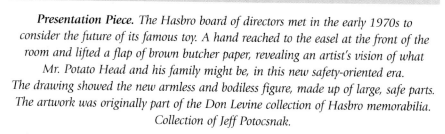

Presentation Piece. *The Hasbro board of directors met in the early 1970s to consider the future of its famous toy. A hand reached to the easel at the front of the room and lifted a flap of brown butcher paper, revealing an artist's vision of what Mr. Potato Head and his family might be, in this new safety-oriented era. The drawing showed the new armless and bodiless figure, made up of large, safe parts. The artwork was originally part of the Don Levine collection of Hasbro memorabilia. Collection of Jeff Potocsnak.*

CHAPTER 8

REMEMBER THE SCREAMING HEADLINES? "DANGER! DANGER! BEWARE OF TOYS!"

*Remember having that doll or truck taken from your fingers
by a fearful parent?
Remember when the words "Be careful!" took the place of
"Have fun!" when kids ran off to play?
The 1970s ushered in a time when toys, for better or worse,
changed utterly.
Changeable Charlie and Wooly Willy would be largely unaffected.
Mr. Potato Head, however, would never be the same again.*

Mr. Potato Head returned to his origins, in a way, in 1975, when he became a part of the "Romper Room" family of toys, by Hasbro Industries. The real highlights of the Hasbro line were now such toys as the Weebles and "Digger the Dog," a toy sniffer-dog that walked alongside a child when revved up with its pull-string.

How did Mr. Potato Head return to his beginnings? By going solo.

Yet it was no longer the same Mr. Potato Head. Not only was he all plastic, but he now measured twice the size of the first toys. This made his facial pieces more acceptable to a safety-minded market. Billed as being a toy for children ages two to six, which was the Romper Room target market, Mr. Potato Head also lost his "fun for the entire family" image so stridently campaigned for, twenty years before.

Of equal significance was the loss of Mr. Potato Head's familiar body, the one that came first with outstretched arms, looking ready to embrace the world, and then in the hands-forward position, introduced when he had to learn to drive. Now he had no separate body at all, only knobs on the bottom onto which the bootie-like feet fit. He also had no hands.

What did he now consist of? The new Mr. Potato Head was a large plastic potato with hats, eyes, eyebrows, ears, glasses, nose, mustache, mouth, and a pipe.

He looked greatly cheerful and engaging. Yet he was a new and different toy, having taken a larger step away from the original than he had in 1964, when the change to plastic had seemed so huge a move.

Not the Same, but Safer. Mr. Potato Head arose in this form from the ashes of the toy-safety furor of the early 1970s, when he had been named one of the least safe toys for children. The change also meant the end of Donald and Bozo in the Potato Head series, and of the Tooty Frooty Friends, who still appeared in packages well into the 1972 season. Collection of Jeff Potocsnak. "Mr. Potato Head," Hasbro Industries, 1972–73.

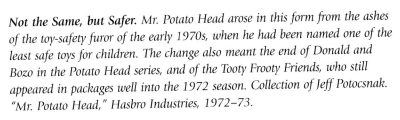

Not Spud, nor Yam. One of the most appealing Potato Head toys of the later 1970s incorporated features of the earlier educational 1970s doll, "Dapper Dan," which had the same name but was otherwise unrelated to Smethport Specialty Co.'s "Dapper Dan" magnetic toy. The toy remained in the funny-face realm by having some interchangeable face parts. Collection of Jeff Potocsnak. Romper Room "Baby Potato Head," Hasbro Industries, 1978.

Meet the New Missus. A rare version, this Mrs. Potato Head came out immediately before the new 1980s version of Mr. Potato Head appeared. Fireman and Sheriff sets were also issued. Collection of Jeff Potocsnak. Hasbro Industries, 1982–83.

TATER TOT AND SUPER SPUD

When "Baby Potato Head" arrived in the late 1970s, he was an obvious take on one of the most famous and successful early-childhood toys of the post-Baby Boom generation—Playskool's "Dapper Dan." This soft-body doll wore durable clothing with flaps that could be unsnapped and then snapped back together. It had zippers to be unzipped, and laces to be tied and untied. A useful tool for teaching young children about getting dressed, the dolls made attractive and charming toys, too.

Baby Potato Head incorporated features of both Mr. Potato Head and Dapper Dan, having a head with interchangeable eyes, mouths, and hats, and a body equipped with zipping and unzipping shirt; pants with a button, snap, and belt buckle; and shoes with laces to tie and untie.

By this time in the 1970s, Mr. Potato Head had not changed from his mid-decade makeover. A bit more flexibility had returned to the toy, in the form of accessory packs. Children could now assemble a "Potato Head Lady," instead of a Mrs. Potato Head, or sheriff or fire chief characters.

Mr. Potato Head continued to be issued in his 1970s form as the 1980s rolled in, with Hasbro advertising that it had sold over 30 million Mr. Potato Head kits through the years.

Introduced in 1980 was the "Super Mr. Potato Head" kit, which made a giant, eleven-and-a-half-inch tall, plastic potato man, more than four inches taller than his already large predecessor. The new "Super" version also came with more accessories, having thirty-two pieces per kit—four pieces more than even the original sets of 1952.

In the early '80s, Hasbro also introduced the distantly related "Thing-A-Ding-Dings," activity toys made of interchangeable parts that could be inserted into a rounded, red plastic body. With it, a child could produce items ranging from a toy airplane to a clock or telephone.

A SUCCESSION OF SPUD HEADS

New versions of Mr. Potato Head had appeared on store shelves, decade after decade, with each change seeming more surprising than the last.

When Mr. Potato Head was about twelve years old, he acquired a plastic potato for a head. When about twenty-two, his head and body merged into a single, larger, potato-shaped piece of plastic. Then, at about thirty-one, he went through a new change, one that turned out to be his final major transformation.

The earliest Mr. Potato Heads were capable of the most expression. Even anger could be expressed. You could create strikingly different characters as well, using different noses and choosing between beady, round, or oval eyes. You could pick out different eyebrows or mustaches. You could put hair on, if you had Mrs. Potato Head or Yam pieces. Since you could also put these features anywhere at all, on any food item you could dig out of the Frigidaire crisper, and since you could choose any shape of vegetable or fruit you wanted—large, small, round, crooked, elongated, warped—the possibilities were truly limitless.

Those possibilities largely disappeared when the plastic potatoes and other "heads" appeared in 1964. In the 1970s, they vanished almost entirely, as Mr. Potato Head's expression was essentially reduced to a single possibility, that of a mature but slightly dumpy and silly-looking vegetable entity, with a permanently pleasant smile and upright, oval, wide-open eyes.

The Mr. Potato Head, who made his debut in 1983 together was a new kind of creature altogether.

Hasbro billed the figures, now part of its "Hasbro Preschool" line, as "goofier and sillier than before," a statement that turned out to be quite true. The flat, oval eyes had become round and bulging. The nose became oval and red. The adult hats became caps. The flesh-tone, stylized ears became more rounded and pink. The mustache, which was discrete and de-emphasized in the '70s, became lushly prominent. The mild smile of the '70s became a silly grin.

With Oscar the Orange Long Gone. The new "Mr. Potato Head Game of the 1970s had only a single character to feature, and never enjoyed the popularity of the similar but much more colorful "Tooty Frooty" game of the previous decade. This was a Sears exclusive. Collection of Jeff Potocsnak. 10" by 10" by 4", Hasbro Industries, 1976.

Look Ma, No Arms. Mr. Potato Head lost some important things in the early 1970s, not least of which were his body, arms, and hands. The version pictured is of the 1970s to early '80s generation of toys, and appeared just before the last new Mr. Potato Head design made its debut. Collection of Jeff Potocsnak. Hasbro Industries, version from 1983–84.

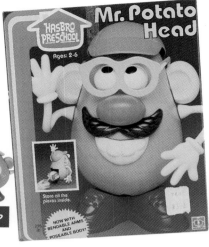

What remained of the Potato Head body changed, too. The legs disappeared entirely, to be replaced by single-unit, oversized tennis shoes affixed to the base of the plastic potato.

Mr. Potato Head had been remade to suit the notions of what a pre-school toy should be. While in his 1950s and '60s incarnations, he displayed enough flexibility to be suitable for an older child's play and even an entertaining gag item for adults, Mr. Potato Head was now firmly fixed as a plaything for preschoolers.

The new Mr. Potato Head of 1983 did have one feature that hearkened back a decade and represented an improvement in terms of the toy's play value. He and Mrs. Potato Head re-acquired hands. This time they appeared at the end of long, bendable arms, which fit into the sides of the plastic bodies.

Unlike previous versions, these new figures, seven and a half inches tall, had almost no flexibility as to their appearance. When you bought the toy, you bought one set of features to make one kind of face.

Hasbro did keep alive the idea of the "Super Mr. Potato Head," still four inches taller than the standard version. This larger toy did include some extra pieces, including the pipe.

In both sizes, the Potato Head toys had a new feature: a door in the back of the plastic potato that opened, turning the body into a storage container for the facial pieces, a sensible innovation anticipated by Tupperware's "Eggsters" of more than a decade before.

Mr. Potato Head's pipe, one of the features that tied every new Mr. Potato Head to the previous version, and especially to that first, striking toy of 1952, had only three more years to go. During the publicity blitz for the Great American Smokeout, Hasbro presented the last plastic pipe to Surgeon General C. Everett Koop, in a symbolic gesture: a potato was giving up its only vice.

In a way, the event finally closed the door on the period of time when the funny-face toy almost reigned over the playroom.

The last leftover of those fabulous '50s were disappearing everywhere.

With the vanishing of the pipe from the toy box, an entire era disappeared.

The 1980s Changeover. Mr. Potato Head regenerated his arms for the new 1980s sets. More than ever before, the toys had a cute look designed to appeal mainly to the youngest children. Collection of Jeff Potocsnak. 6" by 7½" by 4¼", Hasbro Industries, 1983.

All Foam. Some store displays unwittingly evoked the original, foam-headed sets. This 2-foot tall toy-department display was made entirely of foam. This particular figure is missing its ears. Collection of Jeff Potocsnak. Hasbro, late 1980s.

Potato Head Family. No name seemed needed for "Baby Potato Head." The family set came with 33 pieces. Collection of Jeff Potocsnak. Hasbro Preschool "Mr. Potato Head Family," Hasbro Industries, 1985.

Another Egg-Head. In an earlier decade, the "Gollies" series of toys might have been more properly funny-face toys. In the safety-conscious 1970s, however, they had no removable facial parts. Only the small body and the small horse-drawn covered wagon were removable. These pieces could be stored inside the egg-shaped head. Collection of Jeff Potocsnak. 6" by 4" by 4½", "Tex Golly," Questor Education Products Co., 1970s.

AN OBSESSION WITH SAFETY

An alarmist wave, fanned by a good amount of sensationalist journalism, changed the toy world forever in the years from 1969 through the early '70s. When headlines claimed toys were killing children, parents listened. So did politicians.

When the House of Representatives voted on an early toy-safety regulation, it passed the measure unanimously. As a consequence of this political fervor, by the early 1970s toy manufacturers were being regulated under the Federal Hazardous Substances Act, not under the Consumer Products Safety Act.

The President was even granted emergency power, allowing him personally to ban any toy he deemed unsafe. The game introduced by Dynamic Design Industries in 1971 may have been a direct reply. Undoubtedly, in its name alone, it expressed the frustration felt by members of the toy industry: "Who Can Beat Nixon?"

"Children know what toys are all about. Otherwise they wouldn't want them, and play with them," said one representative of the toy manufacturing industry. "It's the parents, the would-be parents and the politicians who no longer understand what it's like to be a child. We'd like to hear from those politicians and consumerists who are speaking against toys today. What toys did they play with, and how did they survive all the so-called hazards involved?"

By the time the statistics were rolled out, revealing that only a handful per thousand of recorded household injuries involved toys, and by the time the testimony was heard that a toy loudly decried for disabling a child was a cheap foreign import and not a toy made in the States, the damage was done, and done thoroughly.

It may well be true that toy manufacturers had not set stringent enough standards for toy safety before the 1970s. Yet it may well be true, too, that the safety standards developed within the toy industry in the late 1960s and early '70s were quite adequate, and not deserving of the rebuff they received from politicians eager to show how aggressively they were on watch.

It is an unquestionable fact that once the hysteria passed, toys were never the same again. More than anything else, the toy-safety scare effectively ended an era in toy-making that extended from the late 1940s through the Baby Boom years, and that produced some of the most memorable toys of all time.

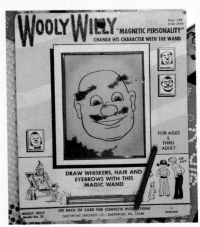

Character Unchanged. The toy whose character could be changed with a Magic Wand remained essentially unchanged. When Smethport revamped "Wooly Willy" to suit the altered regulatory atmosphere of the 1970s, the essential toy remained the same. A few cosmetic changes were made. The toy was now marked for an age group: "For Ages 5 Thru Adult." It also had a "Product Safety and Quality" statement on the back. The "Wooly Willy" shown here appears with other Smethport toys in the background, including "Doodle Balls." Photo by and collection of Mark Rich. 7" by 9", Smethport Specialty Co., 1974 and subsequent years.

Food Selling Food. *In his last incarnation, Mr. Potato Head became involved in food promotions. As did "Dunkie Donut," the move recalled the toy's origins in the "Identikit." Here, one of the authors reveals his true identity while holding up a fast-food cardboard display. Collection of Jeff Potocsnak. Burger King display, 1998–99; mask, late '90s.*

AFTERWORD

For many people, the most familiar funny-face toys will be the most recent ones. "Changeable Charlie" has appeared in reissues from various toy and novelty firms, under the name "Willy Mixtup" and others. "Wooly Willy" magnetic-whisker toys have continued appearing in various forms, including recent key-chains commemorating classic toys. Mr. Potato Head, especially, has enjoyed a resurgence.

While entirely changed in character and appearance in the 1980s, the famous spud-head went on into the 1990s and beyond, and continued to enjoy popular success. He was, after all, Mr. Potato Head. In the 1990s, he appeared in two Walt Disney animated motion pictures, and in numerous books for young children. He inspired a series of tourist-attraction

Mr. Refrigerator Head. *The whole refrigerator could serve as the head with this 15-piece set. It also included a magnet in the shape of a Potato Head outline. Collection of Jeff Potocsnak. "Mr. Potato Head Magnets," Playskool/Hasbro, 1997.*

Bert and Ernie. *Turned one way, the toy made a "Sesame Street" Bert figure. Turned again, the head became Ernie's. Collection of Jeff Potocsnak. "Make-A-Fun Face," Playskool/Hasbro, 1992.*

statues around Rhode Island, and, more recently, a daily comic strip by cartoonist Jim Davis. Fast-food toys and a succession of new kits have also appeared.

People naturally come across these more recent items more often than they luck upon items of the 1970s, '60s, or '50s. Such newer toys provide interesting collecting, and often stimulate people into looking farther back, out of nostalgia and curiosity.

We may never know exactly why funny-face toys have kept entertaining us for so many years.

In them we may see reflections of those crazy uncles, leaning over our cradles in those vulnerable first few weeks of our existences.

Or maybe we just see ourselves.

Twice Baked. Mr. Potato Head finally underwent the transformation into a "Hot Potato" toy in the 1990s, borrowing the basic idea from Ohio Art's plastic 6" toy "Spudsie," of the 1960s. Squeezing this 8"-tall, polyester-filled toy activated the music and voice box inside. Photo by and collection of Mark Rich. "Hot Potato," Parker Brothers/Hasbro, 1995.

Toy Story Mr. Potato Head. *Collection of Jeff Potocsnak. Hasbro, 1995.*

Wooly Wabbit. *Other companies picked up on the magnetic whiskers idea. This "Wonder Whiskers" toy features a famous Warner Brothers face. Collection of Mark Rich. 6" by 8½", "Bugs Bunny Wonder Whiskers." Henry Gordy International, 1989.*

True to Tradition. *These two Hong Kong kits called for real potatoes, evoking now long-gone times. The "Mr. Potato Head" kit is unlicensed, while the "Mr. Spud Head" was released by the nostalgia company Accoutrements. Both sets feature fragile bodies and features much like the original Mr. Potato Head pieces. Mr. Spud Head's nose, however, is oval, as Mr. Potato Head's nose became in the 1980s and '90s. Collection of Jeff Potocsnak, photo by Mark Rich. 2" by 3¼", Unknown manufacturer, probably 1980s and '90s.*

Potato Head Show. These standees came from the set of the "Mr. Potato Head" children's TV show on the Fox Network. The Potato Head Kids had a TV show, too, in the 1980s. Collection of Jeff Potocsnak. Late 1990s.

103

MR. POTATO HEAD AT THE END OF THE CENTURY

1987 — Mr. Potato Head gives up his pipe and becomes official "Spokespud" of the American Cancer Society's "Great American Smokeout."

1989 — "Super Silly Mr. Potato Head" buckets introduced.

1992 — In his 40th year, Mr. Potato Head receives the Presidential Sports Award from the President's Council on Physical Fitness and Sports.

1995 — Appears in Disney feature, *Toy Story*.

1996 — Goes digital on "Mr. Potato Head Saves Veggie Valley" CD-ROM.

1996 — More than 50 million figures have been sold since 1952.

Source: Hasbro "Mr. Potato Head" seller's style guide, 1996.

104

I want to thank my parents Joe and Irene, and my older siblings Jim, John, Joe, and Margie for encouraging me to maintain family baby status and behavior well into adulthood.

And true Irishman Tim Shannon, who encouraged my potato fascination through his own obsessive love of mashed potatoes from an early age.

Thanks, too, to like-minded friends John Melvin, Paul Johanni, Bill Hennen, Patrick Eugene Malloy, and Jim Pederson.

Also, of course, to my wonderful wife, Elizabeth, for encouraging me to have fun in all we do.

And to my kids Ellen, Sophie, and Stephen for letting me play with their toys even though I don't share mine very often.

In my collecting, I have received encouragement from Ellen Holbrook, of Fun1st.com, and Uncle Frank Webster, founder of the Hot Dog Hall of Fame. Thanks also to all the various toy and antique dealers and fellow collectors who have helped me build my collection.

Most importantly, since my collection would never have been shared with the world without his efforts, to my co-author Mark Rich.

– Jeff Potocsnak

Wood figure by Terry Perdue.

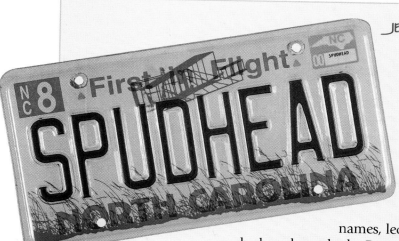

JEFF POTOCSNAK

He clearly remembers playing with Frenchy Fry, Frankie Frank, and Willy Burger in the basement of his Cleveland home. While the older Mr. Potato Head sets around the house belonged to his brothers, these greasy-spoon characters were all his. Teasing at school, where kids called him "Mr. Potato Head," because of a similarity between his and the toy's names, led him into collecting. Since that time, he has always had a Potato Head nearby—in the dorm room at school, on the desk at his various jobs around the country, and now at *home*—*everywhere* in his home. He lives in the Chicago area, and works in human resources.

Jeff's collection must rank as the premiere assemblage of funny-face toys on the funny face of the planet. Without it, this book could never have come about. May his face always be funny.

Thanks especially to my partner in life and collecting, Martha Borchardt. Thanks to my wonderful parents. Thanks to Bill and Mai Larson, for helping me lately be Mr. Beer Head; to Becky Stubbe, for surrendering some of her collection; to Rick Bowes, Scott Edelman, Nalo Hopkinson, and Amy Sheldon, for allowing their memories to become a part of this book; to the fine folk at the farmer's market, for unknowingly contributing; and to Don Gulbrandsen, for special efforts in making this book possible.

Thanks, too, to all of you who have listened to me beating my tin drum on dozens of radio stations around the country about how Mr. Potato Head, not that fashion doll, what's-her-name, was the single toy, if only one must be chosen, that had most universal impact on boys and girls of the Baby Boom generation as a whole. Special thanks to that former storekeeper who talked to me during one call-in show, and agreed with me.

I asked him: "What toy could you not keep on your shelves, back in the '50s?"

He replied, without hesitation: "Mr. Potato Head."

Jeff and I also extend our thanks to Jodi Rintelman, Bill Krause, Sharon Korbeck, and photographers Ross Hubbard and Bob Best for their help in different stages of making this book a reality.

– Mark Rich

Photos by Mark Rich.

MARK RICH

Since he grew up with plastic-headed toys rattling around in "Tooty Frooty" boxes, he probably made his best toy faces with plasticene, or with crayons on paper. He has written two books dealing with toy history: *100 Greatest Baby Boomer Toys* and *Toys A to Z*. He may write some more. He lives in Wisconsin potato-growing country. He does not grow potatoes. He does, however, also write science fiction, rock music, and literary criticism.

Funny-Faced Car. An 18-piece set assembled into the new Mr. Potato Head and his new, blue car. Mr. Potato Head riding his car also appeared on the Mr. Potato Head's Vacation Coloring Book, published by Happy House in the same year. "Mr. Potato Head and His Funny-Faced Car," Hasbro Industries, 1985.

Hamilton Sperr, Portia, ed. *Building Block Art.* Philadelphia, Penn.: Please Touch Museum, 1986.

Culff, Robert. *The World of Toys.* London: Hamlyn Publishing Group, 1969.

Hoffman, David. *Kid Stuff.* San Francisco: Chronicle Books, 1996.

King, Constance Eileen. *The Encyclopedia of Toys.* New York: Crown Publishing, 1978.

McClintock, Inez and Marshall. *Toys in America.* Washington, D.C.: Public Affairs Press, 1961.

Miller, G. Wayne. *Toy Wars.* New York: Random House, 1998.

Rich, Mark. *100 Greatest Baby Boomer Toys.* Iola, Wis.: Krause Publications, 2000.

———*Toys A to Z.* Iola, Wis.: Krause Publications, 2001.

Schroeder, Joseph J., Jr. *The Wonderful World of Toys, Games & Dolls.* Northfield, Ill.: DBI Books, 1971.

White, Gwen. *Antique Toys and Their Background.* New York: Arco Publishing Co., 1971.

Full Family. Box interior. Collection of Jeff Potocsnak. Hassenfeld Bros., 1953.

■ ■ ■

"When I decided to collect Mr. Potato Head, I thought I'd need to find something like ten sets, and then I'd have a complete set. "And then it started."

—*Jeff Potocsnak*

Collection of Jeff Potocsnak.

TIPS FOR COLLECTORS

Collectors of "Mr. Potato Head" and other funny-face toys are in good part collectors of boxes. The boxes were cardboard and not designed to last for years, let alone decades. To find one in good to excellent shape, especially with all the interior inserts intact, becomes a matter of rejoicing—yet another rare object has survived the ravages of time!

Collectors seek the boxes for more than just their rarity, however. As you have seen in example after example in this book, the boxes these toys came in, especially the boxes of the 1950s, are extremely attractive. Colorful, imaginative, and entertaining, they are delightful items unto themselves, even without the pleasant thoughts of childhood and play they evoke.

The plastic pieces that came in these boxes are a bit easier to find. When buying assortments, check for broken tips on the back of the features, and for bodies with the stubs of broken hands in the arms. If the pieces have food residue, soaking them in a weak soap solution should do the trick. If you are playing with them using real vegetables—which we highly recommend—clean the tips afterward with rubbing alcohol.

Store boxes out of direct sunlight. Keep the plastic facial pieces in the foam heads when displaying the kits, especially the ones with cellophane windows. They look fabulous this way. When storing them, however, you might do well to remove the pieces from the foam, since the two kinds of plastic seem to react with each other over time.

Our most important tip, however, is this:

Have fun. Collect for your own pleasure. Don't let collector values get in the way of enjoying these treasures.

Collection of Jeff Potocsnak.

108

THE PRICE GUIDE

The following is meant to be a guide only. Prices for old toys vary greatly from region to region, and from year to year. In the case of prices that may seem remarkably high, all we are saying, in recording them here, is that some collectors have been willing to think in these terms, somewhere in the United States, sometime in the last five or so years as we write this. Bear in mind that collectors who have paid these prices once may never do so again. On the other hand, bear in mind that funny-face toy collecting may still be in its infancy, in which case other collectors may be only too glad to pay these prices.

We have provided few estimated values on items from the 1980s and 1990s, since few of these items command significant collector interest, as of yet.

The values are organized by manufacturer, including "Unknown." German and Mexican sets are listed in this category. "NPF" means No Price Found, and also No Price Guessed.

The prices are for excellent sets in excellent boxes, an ideal rarely achieved.

Photos by Mark Rich.

Disguised as a Kid. Although the mask of a Potato Head Kid, the box for this costume reads, "Mr. Potato Head." A child named Dennis first owned this set. Collection of Jeff Potocsnak. Ben Cooper, 1986.

Potato Head Kids. Collection of Jeff Potocsnak. 24-piece, 15" by 12" puzzle, Milton Bradley Co., 1980s.

Potato Head Kids Game. Collection of Jeff Potocsnak. Milton Bradley Co., 1980s.

Milton Bradley Co.
"Potato Head Kids" game...............................$5
"Potato Head Kids" puzzle...........................$4

Ben Cooper
"Potato Head Kid" costume, 1986 ....$20

Charles M. Crandall
"Crandall's Expression Blocks"
....$125–$150

De Luxe Game Corporation
Magnetic Comic Faces ....$25–$50

Charles William Doepke Manufacturing Company
"Changeable Charlie" ....$30–$40
"Bozo the Clown … Blocks"...............$30–$40

Elmar Products Co.
"Mr. & Mrs. Funny Face" ....$5–$10

Hassenfeld Bros./Hasbro Industries
"Baby Potato Head," 1978 ....$20
"Big Mouth" ....$50–$70
"Captain Kangaroo's Pets" $300
"Dunkie Donut-Head" $150

Hassenfeld Bros./Hasbro Industries, cont.

"Happy Holiday Friends" $210

"Jumpin Mr. Potato Head" $175

"Jumpin Mr. Potato Head," 1967, 5x9 ....$80

"Jumpin Mrs. Potato Head" $175

"Let's Face It" ....$50–$70

"Loony-Kins"...$35–$45

"Make-A-Fun Face," 1992 ....$10–$15

"Merry Milkman" ....$60–$80

"Mr. Magnet Man" $35

"Mr. Potato Head," 1952, cardboard head
....$110

"Mr. Potato Head," 1952, foam head $60

"Mr. Potato Head," 1953, window box......$110

"Mr. Potato Head," driving box, color $90

"Mr. Potato Head," driving box, white sky..$90

"Mr. Potato Head," header bag $35

"Mr. Potato Head," 1962, box $70

"Mr. Potato Head," 1972, last old version ..$35

"Mr. Potato Head," 1972–73 ....$80

"Mr. Potato Head," 1984 ....$30

"Mr. Potato Head," Romper Room $35

"Mr. Potato Head," late 1980s.....................$15

"Mr. Potato Head," costume, 1960 ....$110

"Mr. Potato Head" riding toy, with box $250

"Mr. Potato Head" riding toy, no box........$150

"Mr. Potato Head & His Bucket of Parts," 1987
....$30

"Mr. Potato Head & His Funny-Faced Car" $60

"Mr. Potato Head Eras-O-Picture Book"......$45

"Mr. Potato Head Family," 1985 ....$40

"Mr. Potato Head Game," 1976, Sears $70

"Mr. Potato Head in the Circus" $250

"Mr. Potato Head in the Masquerade" $150

"Mr. Potato Head in the Parade".................$85

"Mr. Potato Head in the Wild West"..........$150

"Mr. Potato Head on the Farm" $85

"Mr. Potato Head on the Moon" $400

"Mr. Potato Head on the Railroad".............$95

"Mr. Potato Head Pencil Case,"
....see "School Days"

"Mr. Potato Head Plus ... Donald Duck"....$75

"Mr. Potato Head Plus ... Bozo" $75

"Mr. Potato Head Pops" $60

"Mrs. Potato Head," 1953, window box....$110

"Mrs. Potato Head," 11" x 16" box, 1959 $400

Walt Disney Mickey Mouse Pencil Case. Photo by Mark Rich. Hassenfeld Bros., probably early 1950s.

109

Sears Exclusive. This Romper Room version of the famous Potato Head duo was a store exclusive, and extremely difficult to find. Collection of Jeff Potocsnak. 8" by 12", Hasbro Industries, 1980.

Loony-Kins. Photo by Mark Rich. Hassenfeld Bros., mid-1950s.

Talking Potato. Collection of Jeff Potocsnak. Hasbro, 1990s.

110

Space Spud. Photo by Mark Rich. Hassenfeld Bros., 1968.

Mr. Potato Head Paint with Water. Collection of Jeff Potocsnak. Happy House/Random House, 1995.

Mr. and Mrs. Potato Head Costumes. Collection of Jeff Potocsnak. Simplicity, 1992.

Hassenfeld Bros./Hasbro Industries, cont.

"Mrs. Potato Head," 1962, box $70

"Mrs. Potato Head," 1972, last old version $35

"Mrs. Potato Head," 1984 ....$80

"Mrs. Potato Head," late 1980s $15

"Mrs. Potato Head" costume, 1960 ....$110

"Mr. & Mrs. Potato Head Combination Kit," 1953 ....$80–$85

"Mr. & Mrs. Potato Head Combination Kit," color box $80

"Mr. & Mrs. Potato Head," with kids, #2006, b&w $120

"Mr. & Mrs. Potato Head," with kids, #2006, color $120

"Mr. & Mrs. Potato Head," 1959, color $130

"Mr. & Mrs. Potato Head," 1959, white sky$110

"Mr. & Mrs. Potato Head Biggest All-New," 1960 ....$375

"Mr. & Mrs. Potato Head," 1962 ....$110

"Mr. & Mrs. Potato Head New Super Giant," 1962 ....$150

"Mr. & Mrs. Potato Head," 1980, Sears $200

"New Super Fun Pak," 1953 ....$80

"New Super Fun Pak," with molded Spud-Ettes bodies, 1954 ....$300

"Picnic Pals," plain box (1999 auction)....$800

"Picnic Pals," individual............................$125

"Potato Head Kids," various, 1985......$12–$15

"School Days Mr. Potato Head Pencil Case," small...$30

"School Days Mr. Potato Head Pencil Case," deluxe ....$25–$35

"Silly Mr. Potato Head," bucket, 1989 ....$20

"Slim Dandy" $175

"Spud-Ettes," circus wagon box, 1953 ......$130

"Spud-Ettes," No. 2010 ....$180

"Spudettes," small window box $120

"Spudettes," header bag $25

"Spudettes," blister card $30

"Super Mr. Potato Head," 1980....................$65

"Tooty Frooty Game" $180

"Tooty Frooty Friends," combined boxes....$80

"Tooty Frooty Friends," individual, regular $40

"Tooty Frooty Friends," individual, window$70

"Tooty Frooty Friends," painted box, 1966 $65

"Tooty Frooty Friends," individual, 1972....$50

Disguised as a Potato—With Only Two Eyes. *Unlike the one-piece suit with the Mr. Potato Head, Mrs. Potato Head's outfit was two-piece, with separate top and skirt. Collection of Jeff Potocsnak. Hassenfeld Bros., 1960.*

Mr. Potato Head Wacky Stack. *This toy allowed changes by turning sections of the Potato Head around, almost as in a combination of Mr. Potato Head and Changeable Charlie. Collection of Jeff Potocsnak. Hasbro, 1998.*

Mr. Potato Head and Friends 3-D Stickers. *Collection of Jeff Potocsnak. Romper Room/Hasbro Industries, 1979.*

Mr. & Mrs. Potato Head. *10th anniversary box. Collection of Jeff Potocsnak. Hassenfeld Bros., 1962.*

Super Mr. Romper Room Head. *Collection of Jeff Potocsnak. 8″ by 12″, Hasbro Industries, 1980.*

Mr. Potato Head. *Collection of Jeff Potocsnak. Hasbro Industries, 1970s.*

Remote Talking Mr. Potato Head. *Collection of Jeff Potocsnak. Hasbro, 1999.*

Potato Head Buckets. *On right, "Mr. Potato Head & His Bucket of Parts," 1987. On left, "Silly Mr. Potato Head Bucket," 1989. Collection of Jeff Potocsnak. Playskool/Hasbro.*

112

Small Potatoes. Some but not all of these 1980s kids had potato-based names: Big Chip, Potato Dumpling, Potato Puff, Slick, Smarty Pants, and Spike. Collection of Jeff Potocsnak. Hasbro Industries, 1985.

Gaston Mfg. Co.
"Blondie & Dagwood Interchangeable" ....NPF
"Bozo the Clown … Blocks"...............$25–$35
"Changeable Charlie," 1950s ....$25–$45
"Dagwood Interchangeable Blocks"...........NPF

Halsam Products Co.
"Changeable Charlie" ....$15–$30
"Changeable Charlie's Aunt" ....$20–$35

Jaymar Specialty Co.
"Popeye's Funny Face Maker" ....$10–$15

Kenner Products Co.
"Doozies"...................................$10–$15
"Popeye Doozies" ....$15–$20

Langwood Products
"Juggle-Head," 1950s...................$35–$45
"Juggle-Head Jr.," 1950s $30

McDonald's
"Potato Head Kids" bag $8

Merit
"Mrs. Potato Head" $60

Multi-State Industries
"Silly Billy"....................................$45

Peerless Playthings Co.
"Mister Funny Face," 1950s $35

Peter Pan Playthings
"Mr. Egg-Bodd," 1960s $70
"Mr. Egg Head," 1950s $90
"Mr. Potato Head," 1950s $100
"Mr. Potato Head," 1968 ....$35
"Mr. Potato Head & Mr. Egg Head"...........$110
"Mr. Potato Head on Safari" $100
"Prairie Potato Head" $120

Pressman Toy Corp.
"Space Faces," 1950s ....$200–$250

Mrs. Potato Head. *Collection of Jeff Potocsnak. Playskool/Hasbro, late 1980s.*

Stuffed Potato. *Collection of Jeff Potocsnak. Hasbro, 1990s.*

113

Mr. Potato Head Rubber Stamp Set. *Collection of Jeff Potocsnak. Pepperwood International Corp. and Hasbro Bradley, 1985.*

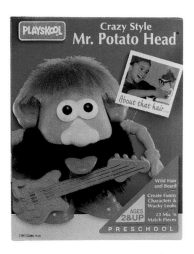

School Days Potato Head Pencil Case. *Photo by Mark Rich. Hassenfeld Bros., mid-1950s.*

Crazy Style Mr. Potato Head. *Collection of Jeff Potocsnak. Playskool/Hasbro, 1994.*

Soft Walkin' Wheels. *"Soft motorized car with a fun walking action." Collection of Jeff Potocsnak. Playskool/Hasbro, 1997.*

Mr. Potato Head Sprinkler. *Collection of Jeff Potocsnak. Hasbro, 1990s.*

Inflatable Mr. Potato Head. *The cloth-bodied inflatable toy stood 19" high. Collection of Jeff Potocsnak. Hasbro, 1996.*

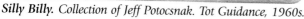

Silly Billy. Collection of Jeff Potocsnak. Tot Guidance, 1960s.

114

Mr. Potato Head glass ornament. Collection of Jeff Potocsnak. Christopher Radko, 1997.

Tin Kin. An appealing magnetic offshoot of the Potato Head line appeared in Hasbro's Romper Room line, with the head being a simple, red tin canister. Facial features and squat body alike held tightly to the tin, which could also serve to hold the pieces. Unlike Mr. Potato Head, "Mr. Magnet Head" had all the flexibility of a 1950s toy. Collection of Jeff Potocsnak. Hasbro Industries, 1970s.

Questor Education Productions Co.
"Tex Golly" $5

Christopher Radko
"Mr. Potato Head" ornament ....$65–$85

The Saalfield Publishing Co.
"New Funmaker Box," 1950s or 1960s $15

A. Schoenhut Company
"'Ole' Million Face," 1920s ....$125–$150

Smethport Specialty Co.
"Dapper Dan," 1950s–60s...........................$15
"Doodle Balls," 1950s–60s ....$5–$15
"High Spy," 1960s $10
"Magnetic Drawing Set," 1974.....................$10
"The Original Wooly Willy," late version $5
"Wooly Willy," 1950s...........................$15–$20
"Wooly Willy," 1970s ....$5–$10

The Tracies Co.
"Make-A-Face" game, 1948 ....$10–$20

Tupperware Toys
"Eggsters" ....$5–$10

Unknown
"Allan Apple" $5
"Funny Face Kit" $5
"Funny Faces" ....$5–$10
"Mr. Funny Face," 1950s ....$5–$10
"Mr. Puddin Head".................................$10–$15
"Tio Papa," Mexican $85
"Mr. Funny Face," West Germany $40
"Mr. Potato Head," Hong Kong...................$15
"Mr. Potato Head," West Germany, '50s/'60s
....$55
"El Señor Patata," Mexican............................$30

Whitman Publishing Co.
"Funny Face," 1950s or '60s........................$15
"Funny Face, Family Game of Fun," 1965
....$8–$12

Dagwood. Photo by Mark Rich. Gaston Mfg. Co., 1951.

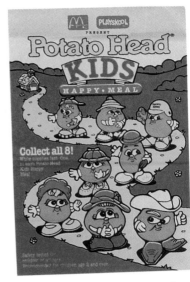

Potato Head Kids Happy-Meal Bag. Collection of Jeff Potocsnak. McDonald's, 1992.

115

Toy Story 2 Mr. and Mrs. Potato Head. Collection of Jeff Potocsnak. Hasbro, 1999.

Plush and vinyl Mr. Potato Head. Collection of Jeff Potocsnak. 6-1/2" high, Giftco, 2000.

Changeable Blocks. Halsam Products Co., 1960s.

Juggle-Head. Collection of Jeff Potocsnak. Langwood Products, 1953.

Prairie Potato Head. Peter Pan, England, mid-1960s. Photo by Mark Rich.

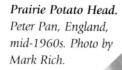

Mr. Egg-Bodd. Collection of Jeff Potocsnak. Peter Pan Playthings, 1960s.

Wooly Willy. Collections of Jeff Potocsnak and Mark Rich. Smethport Specialty Co., 1970s.

Mr. Egg-Bodd. Collection of Jeff Potocsnak, photo by Mark Rich.

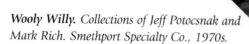

Wrigley Field Special Edition. Collection of Jeff Potocsnak. "Mr. Potato Head," Hasbro, 2000.

Potato of Many Fields. Mr. Potato Head took on the role of golfer, doctor, and fisherman in these sets. He first fished 24 years earlier, as Jumpin Mr. Potato Head. Collection of Jeff Potocsnak. Playskool/Hasbro, 1990.

Mr. Egg Head and "Mr. Potato Head and Mr. Egg Head." Collection of Jeff Potocsnak. Peter Pan Playthings, 1960s.

A NOSTALGIC LOOK AT YOUR FAVORITE TOYS

100 Greatest Baby Boomer Toys

by Mark Rich

Relive your childhood with this nostalgic picture book of toys from your past. You'll reminisce as you look at the photos and read about the history of these toys, whether you're a baby boomer, a collector, or just looking for a fabulous gift. The 100 greatest toys are ranked in popularity and value listings are included for many more. And, if you're not already a collector, you may become one after seeing the values of some of those deep-in-the-closet keepsakes.

Softcover • 8-1/4 x 10-7/8 • 208 pages
250 color photos
Item# BOOM • $24.95

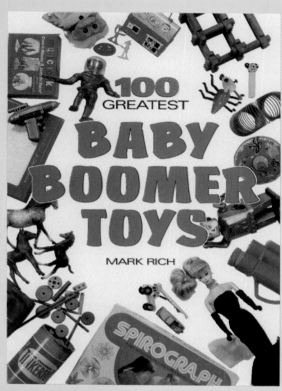

Toys A to Z

A Guide and Dictionary for Collectors, Antique Dealers and Enthusiasts

by Mark Rich

How did Fisher-Price get its start? What company produced cast-iron toys in Freeport, Illinois? And who was Milton Bradley, anyway? The answers to these and hundreds of other questions are in Toys A to Z, a handy pocket reference. Containing thousands of entries covering the colorful world of toys, games, dolls and more. You'll want to refer to it again and again.

Softcover • 6 x 9 • 480 pages
300+ b&w photos and illustrations
Item# TOYD • $19.95

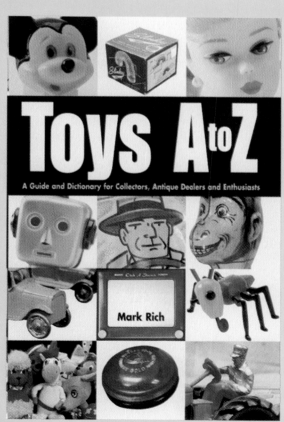

REFERENCE BOOKS FOR COLLECTORS

Antique Trader® Toys Price Guide
edited by Kyle Husfloen, Contributing Editor Dana Cain
This comprehensive toy price guide lists 3,500 toys-from the true antique to the typical collectible–and provides detailed descriptions with current values. Take a close-up look at the major varieties of collectible toys produced during the past 200 years, especially since World War II. Compact and organized alphabetically by category, you'll find it both handy and easy to use.
Softcover • 6 x 9 • 292 pages
400 b&w photos • 16-page color section
Item# ATTP1 • $14.95

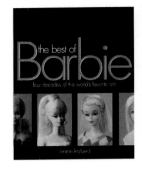

The Best of Barbie®
Four Decades of America's Favorite Doll
by Sharon Korbeck
Enchanting. Gorgeous. Presenting America's favorite doll with striking photography, insightful commentary, and historical tidbits. Come and explore the most sought after and valuable Barbie Dolls from 1959 to 2000 with descriptions and more than 1,200 listings to help you easily identify your dolls and price your collection.
Hardcover • 8-1/4 x 10-7/8 • 256 pages
350 color photos
Item# BBARB • $39.95

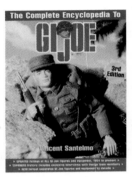

The Complete Encyclopedia to GI Joe
3rd Edition
by Vincent Santelmo
Live the adventures of GI Joe from 1964 to 2000. This updated and expanded edition chronicles the creation of GI Joe, features a complete listing of all figures and accessories released through five decades, contains new interviews with Hasbro's design team, and includes an updated price guide. The NEW collector-friendly format of this invaluable resource for veteran and novice collectors references each GI Joe era by decade.
Softcover • 8-1/2 x 11 • 592 pages
1,000 b&w photos • 48-page color section
Item# JO03 • $27.95

Fisher-Price®
A Historical, Rarity & Value Guide
1931-Present, 3rd Edition
by Bruce R. Fox & John J. Murray
Fisher-Price experts, Bruce R. Fox and John J. Murray have updated and expanded their comprehensive guide to the world's number one toy brand. Features detailed information on more than 3,000 toys, including toy names alphabetized by year, toy identification numbers, number of years made, company history, special remarks, and values ranging from good to mint condition.
Softcover • 8-1/4 x 10-7/8 • 256 pages
50+ b&w photos • 150+ color photos
Item# FIPR3 • $29.95

Marx Toys Sampler
A History & Price Guide
by Michelle L. Smith
In this first behind-the-scenes look at the internal operations and production output of the Marx Toys plant in Glen Dale, West Virginia, you'll learn about Marx toys and the people who produced them. And, you'll find a comprehensive listing, supported by more than 150 photographs, representing over thirty years of lithographed metal and cast plastic toy production–a valuable tool for identifying and dating items in your own collection of Marx Playsets, doll houses, figures, and other toys.
Softcover • 8-1/2 x 11 • 192 pages
150 b&w photos • 16-page color section,
40 color photos • Item# MXTS • $26.95

Saturday Morning TV Collectibles
'60s '70s '80s
by Dana Cain
Zoinks! Do you remember all of the Saturday morning kids programs? This encyclopedia of 1960s to 1980s kids' shows collectibles will certainly refresh your memory. If you're alr a veteran collector, this guide is great, as it features in-depth listings, prices, and photos of your favorite Saturday morni program collectibles. If you're a novice or beginning hobby you'll find your favorite character collectibles and how muc you should pay. More than 3,500 items priced and nearly 1,000 photos.
Softcover • 8-1/2 x 11 • 288 pages • 750 b&w pho
16-page color section, 200 color photos
Item# TOON • $24.95

Standard Catalog of® Farm Toys
Identification and Price Guide
edited by Elizabeth A. Stephan and Dan Stearns
Now you can own the best farm toy price guide on the market. Covering farm toys from the early 1900s to the 1990s with nearly 5,000 listings and photographs and over 12,000 values, you can identify, price, and catalog your entire collection. Featuring photographs from the collections of Bob Zarse, Eldon Trumm, and the National Farm Toy Museum, this is the only guide you will need.
Softcover • 8-1/2 x 11 • 448 pages
6,000+ b&w photos • 16-page color section
Item# FARMT • $29.95

The Ultimate Roy Rogers Collection
Identification & Price Guide
by Ron Lenius
"Happy trails to you..." in this comprehensive identification and price guide to Roy Rogers, Dale Evans, Gabby Hayes, Trigger, and Bullet collectibles. More than 1,000 photos feature rare and vintage collectibles from 1939 to 1960. Also includes item descriptions, pricing information, and a special interview with Roy and Dale's son, Dusty Rogers.
Softcover • 8-1/4 x 10-7/8 • 208 pages
1,000 color photos
Item# ROYR • $24.95